FISHING
WITH
TARDELLI

FISHING
WITH
TARDELLI

A MEMOIR OF FAMILY
IN TIME LOST

NEIL BESNER

Published by ECW Press
665 Gerrard Street East
Toronto, Ontario, Canada M4M 1Y2
416-694-3348 / info@ecwpress.com

Cover design: Sophie Paas-Lang
Back cover map: Mattos, F. Jaguaribe Gomes De. *Planta da cidade do Rio de Janeiro: obedecendo á divisão da cidade em districtos municipaes.* Rio de Janeiro: Representante-depositario Julien Derenne, 1910. Map. https://www.loc.gov/item/2012593131/.

LIBRARY AND ARCHIVES CANADA CATALOGUING IN PUBLICATION

Title: Fishing with Tardelli : a memoir of family in time lost / Neil Besner.

Names: Besner, Neil Kalman, 1949- author.

Identifiers: Canadiana (print) 20210389796 | Canadiana (ebook) 20210389834

ISBN 978-1-77041-634-5 (softcover)
ISBN 978-1-77305-940-2 (ePub)
ISBN 978-1-77305-941-9 (PDF)
ISBN 978-1-77305-942-6 (Kindle)

Subjects: LCSH: Besner, Neil Kalman, 1949- | LCSH: Besner, Neil Kalman, 1949—Family. | LCSH: Besner, Neil Kalman, 1949—Childhood and youth. | LCSH: College teachers—Canada—Biography. | LCGFT: Autobiographies. | LCGFT: Creative nonfiction.

Classification: LCC PS8603.E77453 Z46 2022 | DDC C813/.6—dc23

This book is funded in part by the Government of Canada. *Ce livre est financé en partie par le gouvernement du Canada.* We acknowledge the support of the Canada Council for the Arts. *Nous remercions le Conseil des arts du Canada de son soutien.* We acknowledge the support of the Ontario Arts Council (OAC), an agency of the Government of Ontario, which last year funded 1,965 individual artists and 1,152 organizations in 197 communities across Ontario for a total of $51.9 million. We also acknowledge the support of the Government of Ontario through the Ontario Book Publishing Tax Credit, and through Ontario Creates.

ONTARIO ARTS COUNCIL
CONSEIL DES ARTS DE L'ONTARIO
an Ontario government agency
un organisme du gouvernement de l'Ontario

Canada Council   Conseil des arts
for the Arts   du Canada

Canadä

PRINTED AND BOUND IN CANADA   PRINTING: MARQUIS   5 4 3 2 1

MIX
Paper from
responsible sources
FSC® C103567

For Gail

"*Of course I may be remembering it all wrong after, after — how many years?*"

— ELIZABETH BISHOP, "SANTARÉM"

"*You must not forget anything.*"

— PHILIP ROTH, *PATRIMONY*

MARINHEIRO
MANUEL
TARDELLI

I was twelve the first time I went fishing with Tardelli on the *Moby Dick*, twenty-four feet, lapstrake, the used boat my stepfather, Walter ("Unca" in those early years), had bought, he told us the first day we came aboard, as a "stepping-stone." He was right. His boats got newer, bigger, made to order. His last one, lost on a reef twenty-five years ago, was fifty-two feet.

That Brazilian winter weekday afternoon when I was twelve, I watched Tardelli steal twenty-five litres of gas from another boat by sucking on a thin rubber hose, spitting out the first gout, and siphoning the rest into the *Moby Dick*. Out of sight of the main marina, the *Moby Dick* slipped away, clandestine, from the back docks of the Iate Clube do Rio de Janeiro with three other sailors — that's what they were called, Brazilians who had washed up into these jobs taking care of these boats — "marinheiros," mariners — and headed out into the bay.

Like almost all of the marinheiros at the yacht club, none of these three could swim. Nor could Tardelli.

When I told Walter (Unca in those years, as I have said) maybe a year later about the gas thefts, he told me I was observing honour among thieves. That sounded fine. At thirteen, fourteen, I was Tardelli's ally, without knowing in which battle, which war, fighting for whom.

I spent my four years of high school in Stamford, Connecticut, at a Jewish boarding school. I came home to Brazil each Christmas for two weeks and each summer for three months, June through August. Thirteen, fourteen, fifteen, sixteen, fishing with Tardelli.

I fished with Tardelli in Rio, in and around the bay. We fished for bluefish. We fished with handlines, thick nylon line wrapped around a board. This type of fishing, called puxa puxa in Portuguese (poosha poosha, or pull, pull), has largely vanished now.

Bluefish continue to inhabit every ocean, but in the polluted bay in Rio, they are now much scarcer.

Tardelli died in 1991. I did not go to his funeral; I am not sure that he had one.

Tardelli could not have been more different from my stepfather, his employer for over thirty years. As I knew he would if such a thing were to happen, Walter called me in Winnipeg from Rio to tell me Tardelli had died. In matters such as these Walter has been nothing short of dutiful, predictable. Reasonable.

Thinking of Kafka's *Letter to His Father*, a few weeks

after Tardelli died, I wrote Walter a sorrowing denunciation of six single-spaced pages. I told him that unlike Tardelli, he was inscrutable; I told him that he was unknowable. I also told him that of course I knew that I would never have met Tardelli, never have come to Brazil, never have lived that fabled life had it not been for him.

Five years later, I made the mistake of giving Walter the letter in Rio. The next day he returned it to me with satisfaction. "You love me," he announced.

To Tardelli's peers he went by his last name; he was one of the few who did not have a nickname. However, the woman who called him to the telephone over the loudspeaker at the yacht club always repeated his name once, the second time rising on the last syllable of his first name: "Marinheiro Manuel Tardelli, Marinheiro ManuEL Tardelli." In memory her voice is measured, warm and singsong, but also officious.

Tardelli calls up no ache, anger, or regret.

I've always believed that Tardelli's name meant he was, like many Brazilians, of Italian descent, but now I'm not sure. I was never in his small house in Vila Kennedy, a state-sponsored development project named after JFK in the tough west of Rio, now drug battle scarred, that took him two hours to get to by bus and train from the yacht club. I met his stocky wife once when she came from those hours away to bring him something. I met one of his sons, Luis, a bitter young man in his twenties who worked at the club for a few months and came fishing with us once on my boat. When I asked him — told him? — to move the beat-up wooden fishbox, he sneered. "Sim senhor, o senhor que manda." Yes, sir, you're the boss. I got it the second time. Tardelli laughed, face away from me.

Tardelli spoke no English save to mock me or, when we were alone, to mock my stepfather. I taught him "seagull." "Sai gol," he laughed. I taught him "fish." "Feesh." He told me that when my stepfather got angry, the back of his neck became a "pescoço vermelho," turned red. He told me that my stepfather had "um medo filha da puta de morrer," a son of a bitch fear of dying. When we were out fishing alone, he mimicked my stepfather on the days when he'd ask Tardelli to take us back to the yacht club for no apparent reason: "Não bom, Manoel, Iate Clube, Iate Clube," no good, Manuel, exaggerating his employer's stilted Portuguese.

Tardelli was never in an airport, never got on an airplane. He disbelieved in flight. In late August each year when we said goodbye for the year he would blow into the palm of his hand: "Vai te, filha da puta," go, you son of a bitch, laughing. He insisted that I do a proper job of wrapping the fish in newspaper bound with fishing line to take home in the evening; he insisted that I take apart my clumsy scrunch and do it again, properly.

He mimicked my posture, head down "like a turtle." One June I found a Christmas postcard in his locker, intended for me but abandoned — the only time I ever saw evidence Tardelli could write. The implications of an address somewhere he barely believed in might have dissuaded him. I was sixteen. Holding the postcard in my hand, I became teary-eyed. I never mentioned this to Tardelli or to anyone else.

Tardelli lusted after and then seduced the cook at home. I never discovered how they'd met. "Speak to me of Floriana," he'd say to me when we were out in the bay. "My cock gets hard just hearing her name." In Portuguese this sounded better. My mother called him Lady Chatterley's Lover, and he was truly handsome. For her and Walter he shaved with soap in his locker, wore carefully pressed whites and clean sneakers. He fished with me in torn shorts, bare-chested and barefoot. I have photos of him in both costumes. They are not contradictory. That would be too simple.

Those Brazilian winters, going fishing with Tardelli in Rio began with lounging carefully along the street near our rented house in Leblon where the cream and blue lotação, the Urca-Leblon bus, passed. There were no bus stops then and the bus didn't stop fully; you flagged it down and swung on with just the right admixture of casual authority.

The driver shifted gears with dramatic sweeps of the arm. His little fingernail was sharpened and polished. He banged the bus down the street, and I dreamed out the window for forty minutes until we got to Urca. I swung off the bus and landed on my feet as per unspoken rules. I was fourteen.

I found Tardelli with Elias, Senhor Elias Abreu, or Marilí, from the Amazon, sitting in the sun on the small step outside Tardelli's locker, eating rice and beans and a hard-boiled egg out of tin boxes. We had a cigarette. I was learning to flick the ash as Tardelli did from the unfiltered Continentals he smoked, a finger brushing ash from the tip. He walked to the edge of the dock and looked down.

"Clear and cold. No good." Cold water meant bad fishing.

"Let's have coffee first, then we'll go," Elias said, and on our way to the sailors' bar, we met Poporoca from Portugal, who slapped me on the back and got his pail with his lines in it and his hooks hanging around the edges and his sack and knife. He walked with us down to the bar and we sat inside on the marble benches, drank strong black coffee, and ate buttered rolls. Tardelli went to the water cooler for a long drink, and we walked by Cabo Verde in the fish shop and promised him we'd bring him something.

It was close to three. The *Moby Dick* was ready down at the hangars, out of sight. The wind came from the east, the boats anchored outside the marina pointed their prows in at Urca mountain with Sugarloaf beside it. We idled out whistling the seagull sound, which meant "tá grosso," it's thick, the fish were there. The empty fishbox was streaked with dried blood and chippy with dried scales and the white paste that the fish vomited when they were full of minnows.

When we left to fish on those salty mid-sixties afternoons, sun mid-sky and a gentle wind from the east, Tardelli, mock ceremonial, mock reverential, would slow down to acknowledge the small statue of São Pedro, patron saint of fishermen, on our way out and again on the way back in the gathering dusk. "Obrigado, São Pedro," he murmured, crossing himself.

São Pedro then as now stands on a small reef. In memory, he has never had the upper half of his raised right arm. São Pedro was clothed then in rusting green. Now the state has gilded him in cheap gold. Tardelli was never Catholic, never religious, always spiritual. The slim white herons that now perch on São Pedro's head wouldn't have dared when he was more properly clothed and rusting.

We waved to the women sitting cross-legged on the stone wall over the rocks as we picked up speed again and moved past Urca and the old man anchored at the point. He was there every good day. We came to the entrance of the bay with our lines stretched out behind us to straighten them, and the ocean opened wide in front of us. The east wind sent small whitecaps in, and the little white gulls with red beaks that cried like lost children were dancing over a stretch of water between the Fort of São João in the middle of the entrance and the Fort of Santa Cruz on the north side. Early one morning Tardelli and I caught ten big bluefish there.

We headed out to the Fort of Imbuí with its long low white clapboard houses on the beach and its big guns on the cliff, and the islet offshore where the bluefish sulked in the coffee-coloured water.

Poporoca sat on the deck seamy-faced, with one gold tooth. His dirty blue shirt was open at the chest and his cap was pulled down hard against the wind. He sharpened a hook and looked up at us with the sprig of green that he always carried tucked behind one ear, and told us, "Of the three of you, I'll fuck two."

Tardelli laughed. "Of the three, I'll fuck three." Elias looked at me. "The old ones are talking again. Of the two of them, I'll fuck two." Then he showed me the calloused open palm of his hand and crushed out his cigarette on it. "For luck."

Tardelli started to sing one of his arias, and Marilí and I turned it into "Cielito Lindo" and repeated the "ai, ai, ai, ai." Poporoca shook his head at us.

The sun was still high in the sky over Sugarloaf but it was starting to go light red as the afternoon took away the noonday glare and the water began to go calm as the wind died down. It would stop for a moment at dusk and then breeze from the southwest for a time before it turned north for the night. All night the wind came from the north and chilled the lovers on the beaches and then freshened the morning and made the sailboats turn their gull prows out to the Fort. The next day we'd watch the wind. If it didn't circle to the east by mid-afternoon, it was likely to go straight southwest and bring cold and rain and raise up the waves. If it blew for too long, the bay got rough and the cargo ships went horsing out to sea. You couldn't hide from the wind except behind Cotunduba Island, where there were seldom any fish, although one day our boat caught one hundred and forty-seven there, and Tardelli stopped after ten fish because he was sick.

We slowed down and idled in close to the rock at Imbuí, on the southwestern point, where sometimes there were groupers, and we lay there and waited to see if the soldiers from the fort would fire shots in the air and wave us away. We watched how the boat rode the current and looked at the colour of the water and felt the strength of the tide. Tardelli put his lure down, took it out, and held it against his cheek to see how cold it was at the bottom.

We watched for the dolphins that came and rode herd on the fish and cut them to pieces. We looked for shark fins and rays. When the rays jumped, it meant the water was cold and the fishing was bad. One winter, the bay was cold for a long time and we came back with five, six fish a day, sometimes none at all. That winter the rays jumped a lot, making tremendous splashes with their wings as they came down. You could see the tumult in the ocean from far off. One ray sunned itself just off the point of the Fort of São João on the protected side, with the tips of its two wings cutting through the water at least six feet apart so that at first it looked like two sharks, until the great flattened oval mouth came into view and it swirled away from the boat.

That cold winter, Tardelli caught two or three big groupers. To catch a grouper the way we fished was to be lucky. They're bottom fish, and so it was a question of the lure falling right next to the mouth and the grouper being hungry. It felt like a bottom snag at first. Then the line began to come up, very slowly, stretched down against the side of the boat. The grouper continued to pull straight down until it came close to the surface, where it tried to swim away. One afternoon at Imbuí, Tardelli caught one of 7 or 8 kilos, a map of yellow and white and brown, large mouth agog, gills working slowly and steadily in the box. Another boat came alongside and bought it. When we came back that evening the grouper was lying on the dock, still alive, and the man who had bought it was looking down at it with his arms folded, explaining how hard he had fought it.

Tardelli scowled at his line stretching out quickly. It popped and throbbed between his fists. He looked at us. "It's because I was thinking about Floriana."

Elias laughed at him. "What about the money she wanted for the dentist?" The money Tardelli told her it was his greatest wish to give her, she'd come to the right man. "She spoke about money, and it ruined everything. I told her that if she needed money, I was the one, I was the man, and that was it. My cock collapsed when it heard 'money.'"

Sometimes the water went light green and the sun picked out sparkling crystal points in the waves. The bluefish lay at the bottom grim and tight-mouthed. That water could bear little but its own absent dance of bright gilt and green. The sky was far up, too blue, empty. Time stopped the sun and the wind came blind and impersonal. We trolled out in the open, lines trailing. Nothing.

Cargo ships drifted in and out of the bay at a distance. We saw a submarine and joked about the Brazilian navy. Straight north, marking the northeastern limit of the outer bay, lay Ilha do Pai, Father's Island, and Ilha da Mãe, Mother's Island, with Island of the Son sheltered between. Father's Island is largely bare rock, a few scattered palms clinging to its slopes and a small reef jutting out from the northeast point. When the ocean was quiet the waves washed low around the rocks, green and white and faintly foam-struck. When it got rougher, we looked from Imbuí and the southwest point whitened and then vanished, and the ocean in between looked rumpled. It was hard then to judge distance, and the salt smell was stronger and heavier. The boat yawed. The black vultures, the urubus that lived on all the islands, soared high long and lazy above the palms.

The southwest wind came from behind the mountains that ranged the coast and greyed the sky and massed the clouds heavy with rain and swung the boats in towards the beach at Botafogo, silent white forms on the water, like resting gulls. From the dock we watched the palm trees on the lower edge of Sugarloaf. If they were bending into the mountain's face and the fronds were shaking, we knew not to go, because outside the wind would be eating the waves. The old trawlers would all be riding at anchor inside the entrance to the bay, and the Fort of São João would be washed over with dull white waves slamming across its rock form, long cold slaps of iron driving themselves over the fort to stream back down, ocean that took colours away from their names and buried the dye deep in herself.

The morning was half gone. Tardelli and I were trolling up and down at Father's Island on the southeast point where the sharks were. We were watching a canoe with an old man in it. We saw him tense up and begin to give out line. Then the canoe started to move as the fish carried him. We circled around him, keeping our distance and looking away because the canoe people thought we put evil eyes on them and they swore at us. We wheeled around to keep the canoe in sight as he brought the fish up, hanging half in and half out along the side of the canoe, and we heard the repeating flat thump of the club as he killed the shark, still hanging over the side. He took a long drink from his water bottle and sat, slumped. Weeks later another large shark glided by us there, back fin slicing just a few feet from where we stood. Tardelli swore at it, threw his lure at it.

Once we saw a lost penguin at the mouth of the bay, come up from far south. It dove every time we came near until Marilí grabbed it and put it in a sack. "Este é um pinguin? Bom dia, Senhor Pinguin!" This is a penguin? Good morning, Mr. Penguin! It scrabbled furiously in the sack. We let it go.

I went to Father's Island alone once in the small boat and found the fish hungry off one point and caught twelve. I got too excited and threw the matchbox into the water, holding the match in my hand after lighting a cigarette. Like Tardelli one morning at the Fort of Santa Cruz, when

I had caught eleven fish and he got flustered changing lures and threw the new one into the water without tying it on.

Memories branching endlessly, but no tree. Wallace Stevens: "There is no wing like meaning." Or memory as lightning, a scimitar flash.

We reminded Tardelli of his throwing the new lure away at Santa Cruz on the days when it was too rough or rainy to go out, and we sat inside his locker and poured heated lead into the wooden mould that one of the carpenters had made for us. We placed a length of wire in the mould, doubled on itself to form an eye at each end. The lead cooled around the wire in the long bullet shape of the lure. We trimmed the edges while the lead was still hot. When twenty or thirty were ready we painted them, blue, yellow, white with blue spots. We crimped a skirt of nylon hair, yellow, white, blue, mixed, to the bottom of the lure with fine wire, and then a hook was clamped in the eye so that the hair hung around it. The different colours had their names — the clown, the killer. We hung them around the pail with the store-bought lures.

The biggest bluefish I ever saw came on a hot Saturday afternoon at Imbuí. Tardelli and I were waiting for the tide, and the fish came alive. We had caught seven or eight when Tardelli swore.

"I've caught bottom." He began to wrap his line back onto the board so that he could hold that and not cut his fingers. He braced himself against the side of the boat and held the board out over the water. Then the line began to give a little and he threw down the board when he had enough slack and pulled the line up slowly. At first we thought it was a big grouper. Then a large blue-white shape swam broadside into view, the lure — a silver zigzag — trailing from one side of the huge open mouth, teeth showing, and Tardelli whispered, "She's the queen of them all," and slowly lifted her out and draped her in the box. Her tail and more hung over one side, her body beaded with drops of water.

Tardelli struck another big bluefish like the queen at Imbuí a few weeks later that summer and fought with it for a long time. When he brought it in close and leaned down slowly to take the lure in one hand, the fish lifted its head out and shook it, looking at us, gills flared red and wide, and the line broke at the knot and the fish turned over and slowly swam down and away.

The first afternoon I went out, the *Moby Dick* with her high freeboard pitched ungainly over the long afternoon swells. We went out to the green buoy that marked where the *Magdalena* lay, a cargo ship that ran aground on a reef and then sank in the middle of the bay some thirty years earlier. The story we heard was that she was carrying a cargo of sugar.

The green buoy sang and moaned in the wind. There was a slow whirlpool directly above the sunken ship, coloured differently from the water at its edges. The ship's masts rose high off the bottom and you could get snagged among them halfway up your retrieve and think you had a big fish on.

The line stretched tighter until it began to sing and then it snapped as the boat rode with the current, and you cursed and said, "I was just stretching the line." Some late afternoons there would be ten, fifteen fugitive boats from the club, and the canoe fishermen, all making their passes with the tide over the dead ship, coming around again when they'd drifted too far off, everyone watching the others for signs of fish.

On the way back that first time, the waves rose blue-black behind us and ran under the stern. I went down to put on my socks and shoes. Poporoca came in and asked if I was afraid. I was. I said no. The waves rose high over the stern and the *Moby Dick* performed what they called the "jacaré," the alligator, burying her nose in the black water, shuddering up to slide down another crest. When we rounded the point at the Fort of São João with the lights from the city shining over the darkening water and sending glimmers of white and yellow across at us, Elias yelled, "Lights, you bastards!" at the trawler anchored just inside the point in the dark so that we almost rammed her. Tardelli laughed. "That's how they die so young."

At the Fort the big brown and white gulls were nesting in their holes in the rock. The little white gulls, trinta-reis, thirty pieces of silver, had gone out to the far islands for the night. The bats and the swallows were circling out from their little caves near the water. In the shelter around the point the water was calm, and the electric sign on the mountain beside us announced, in running red lights, the weather for the next day: "Unstable, with rain, and temperature in decline." The six o'clock news ran across the face of the mountain in bright tracks reflected on the water. The ghost white of the anchored boats came up on us, masts hanging in the sky as we slanted off towards the hangar. We eased in reverse toward the dock, someone at the prow with the anchor, another at the stern to throw a rope up to whoever was waiting for fish. Tardelli reversed the engine in short bursts, cutting off so that we slid to a stop with the anchor holding and the rope knotted around the bollard.

Now the bargaining began, with the "seagulls" all standing around looking at the fish on the dock. Tardelli pretended he didn't see anyone, ambled around the pile, lit a cigarette.

"Poporoca, Senhor Abreu, take your fish." Tardelli said he's not taking any fish today and then they started. "Tardelli, sell me a good fish," said Turk the baker, pedalling up to us with hot bread on his bicycle cart. "Here's our cousin the Turk, what does the Turk want, I know, the Turk wants fish," Tardelli said. The Turk got off his bicycle to look at the fish and gave us fresh rolls. Tardelli gave him a fish when everyone had gone.

Cats slunk through the shadows. Now and then a figure ambled past Tardelli's locker with a wave and the red eye of a cigarette and an airline bag slung over one shoulder.

All of this — the ambling figures in the evening, the Turk on his bicycle cart, the silent cats — occurred and now recurs. The movements unfold decorously in time slowed, then in time slowly flowing. This motion and its progress and regress are like those of the waves on the beach at Ipanema, at Leblon, that I watched unfurling one upon the other when I was in my twenties and thirties and forties and trying to understand time, because I thought then that I could understand time. I thought the waves could teach me. I thought then that if I could understand time, perhaps I could fathom memory. I thought, then, that the variation in the repetition of every wave's unfurling stood for something vital, something unique about time. I thought, then, of Mr. Ramsay in *To the Lighthouse*, who would never arrive at the understanding he was seeking. Now, it is enough to watch the waves furl, unfurl. To contemplate them. To contemplate.

The fish for home were wrapped properly in newspaper. We strolled down the docks in the dark past the sailboats and the pier stretching out grey against the dark, past the clubhouse where the nursemaids sat watching the members' children, and Elias nudged Tardelli. "Just mention Floriana. It still grows, don't worry," Tardelli murmured. We said good night to Jorge the barber in his shop, soon to die unexpectedly. "Jorge fechou," Tardelli told me, laughing, when I got back the following summer. Jorge closed. Eight or nine years later, "Poporoca fechou," with a warmer laugh. Poporoca used to tell Tardelli that he knew how to fish once, but he forgot. Tardelli laughed.

We left the yacht club through the gate for the sailors, and we walked down the street to the short bridge that arched low over another basin, just under the mountain, where the fishermen kept their canoes. We stopped at the little bar there for a coffee, then walked out to lean on the seawall while we waited for our buses. Below us a man sat over a small fire on the rocks with a tin can filled with mussels beside him, holding a handline wrapped around a Coke bottle and watching it disappear into the dark.

Other buses rolled by. The ocean glimmered white against the rocks beneath us. Tardelli told Elias about the man who was run over the day before by the train. Elias asked him if the man was killed; Tardelli said no, he got up and said, "Wow, what a heavy train." "Funny man," Elias said. They swung onto the bus that would take them to the train station.

My smaller Urca-Leblon bus lurched around the corner, and I swung on with my package of fish. The woman beside me looked at the tail coming out of the newspaper and then looked at me and smiled. I kept my eyes down. An hour later I jumped off the bus onto Venâncio Flores, crossed the canal, and started up my street. The crazy maid who lit candles on the street corner and talked to herself, staring at something, was muttering in the middle of the street.

The gate stood white against the red steps leading up to the house. The fake lantern above the front door was warm and yellow in the night air, which carried the light sweet smell of the frangipani trees. I went in the back way and hid the fish in the kitchen. My mother could not stand the sight or, worse, the smell of fish; she forbade them in the house. Outside, the crickets sang. The streetlights warmed the corners, dark in between the crickets.

The crickets paused to listen. American cars sounded

24

American. The lush brown eye of the night earth, the moist leaves — they watched and listened. They heard the hydro-matic click and purr of Park, the silence after the engine was shut off and ticked over twice. A car door shut, metal on metal. There were measured steps up to the gate and the scratch of a key in the lock. There was the controlled rasp of shoe leather. Walter was home.

At eighteen I had been in LA at university, at USC, for two years. It was 1968. Walter stood with me one night in mid-June, near the old wooden warehouses and whorehouses at the downtown dock in Rio on another eve of departure, in a fine Brazilian winter mist so that I was wearing the navy peacoat then in style. I had only come to Brazil to sail north on one of his cargo ships. The *Delilah*, 12,800 tons, sister ship of the *Diana*, loomed metallic and dark grey above us.

I wanted to throw my arms around him. My heart banged in my head, "Please Unca, I'm going crazy."

No words, nor anything else passed between us, and I made it on board.

I said another goodbye to Tardelli a year later, August of 1969, when I was more profoundly lost. I had begun by then to understand these as ritual fading farewells. We stood on the cement dock in the dark at the yacht club, outside the hangar, smoking and looking out across the water at Flamengo and the downtown lights in the flickering city.

I was flying back to California that night; my brother was returning to the University of Miami. Within a year, both of us would be back in Montreal, refugees.

In an hour, Walter would drive me and my brother to the airport. In the car, I would tell him from the back seat that I was thinking of leaving school. There was a pause of one beat. "That's not very smart, is it?" It was one of the few times I had heard an edge in his voice, one of the rare indications that he was subject to irritation.

When my brother and I were seated aboard our flight, I discovered I was crying; my brother asked me why but I couldn't say. Four months later, he flew to LA to bring me back to Montreal after I drove my car into the desert outside Barstow, California, and left it there after speaking with God at night from the top of a low hill I'd scrambled up. A rattlesnake clattered unseen at my feet. Forty years later when I described that evening, God and what He'd said, the snake, the stars, to a psychologist in Winnipeg, he asked me if I had heard of vision quests. But by then I was thinking of Spinoza: "All things are alive." I was thinking of Cohen: "God is alive. Magic is afoot." A Winnipeg friend said to me: "Sometimes the Universe winks at you."

Like many Brazilian men of his time, Tardelli had many women, many children. That night on the dock in 1969 he told me "Eu tenho uma porrada deles espalhado por aí," I have a bunch of them scattered out there. He was half proud, half rueful, all Brazilian. I uttered some querulous complaint. He glanced at me. "Você é jovem, tem muito a aprender." You're young, you have a lot to learn.

No one had ever said such a thing to me.

I hear him now through a scrim of years that smell of saltwater and unfiltered cigarettes.

"Marinheiro Manuel Tardelli, Marinheiro ManuEL Tardelli," the woman sings over the loudspeaker.

I've named my boat here in Lake of the Woods after him.

SENHOR VALTER

I was fifteen, and I am seventy. Some time in between I've read Lowry's *Ultramarine*. But you can't live your life as if it were a novel and you can't read a novel as if it were your life. You cannot, and you must not. I've never understood this. I've always understood this.

Time is eddying and shimmering like water. It's Brazilian winter, mid-July 1965, mid-afternoon, Rio, *boca da barra*, the mouth of the bay. Brazilian winter? In whose cartography of time imagined as space — looking down, or looking up — are the seasons reversed? From which time, in what place?

I was fifteen and I was put on board. I boarded. I'm aboard one of Walter's cargo ships, the *Ponta Negra*, for forty-five days, the rest of that North American summer.

For most Brazilians who know him, "Senhor Valter" is my stepfather Walter's name in Brazil, where he has lived now for going on sixty-five years.

He continues in Rio, cheerful, in his late nineties. He has known me since my birth; I have known him since I was six. That, to begin, is how we were. We have not made very much progress since.

"Mr. Walter" is not an accurate translation. Accuracy has nothing to do with it. "Senhor Valter" signifies the deference headed towards obeisance conferred by Brazilians upon a foreigner with means. "Senhor Valter" signifies a verbal Brazilian bending of the knee. My writing "Senhor Valter," however, signifies my complicity.

Complicity with whom? I'm not Brazilian, although in Brazil I am taken for one. I am fluent in Portuguese, but this is dangerous territory. To escape from English into Portuguese, from Canada into Brazil, from Senhor Valter — himself already at one remove from Montreal, already an ersatz father — to Tardelli: this is seismic territory. This is abandonment and betrayal. In English, it is to become more truly lost.

Senhor Valter's vocabulary in Portuguese is excellent, more extensive than mine, but unlike me, the moment he speaks in Brazil he is given away. Addressing Tardelli, his dignified and modulated "O, Manoel" instantly identifies Senhor Valter as a foreigner, an only son born in 1922 in the small town of Prostějov, birthplace in 1859 of Edmund Husserl, in then-Czechoslovakia. Senhor Valter's family moved to Zagreb when he was six months old. They moved to England before the war broke out. He was a teenager.

I like to think that his fluidity at crossing borders had begun by the time they left Zagreb after his Bar Mitzvah.

I liked his story about Mr. Billinghurst at the public boarding school Senhor Valter attended in England before the war. Mr. Billinghurst hit him smartly on the top of the head with a book, punishment for the boy's lateness in joining the morning lineup. Senhor Valter responded violently. Perhaps this was what my mother meant when she referred to his "Yugoslav temper." He charged Mr. Billinghurst and punched him hard in the stomach, eye-level. He told me that Mr. Billinghurst doubled over. For this act Senhor Valter was expelled.

In Brazil now at breakfast I often remind Senhor Valter of Mr. Billinghurst, the book descending on the head, his charging Mr. Billinghurst and punching him as hard as he could, Mr. Billinghurst doubling over, the expulsion. In this safe territory for us, Senhor Valter laughs with me. We seek this territory, perennially.

There is another anecdote from his younger years in Zagreb, another small oasis where we can laugh together. On the evidence, his mother might also have had a Yugoslav temper. Sitting in their Zagreb apartment's kitchen, his mother, her brother, and Walter, the brother complained to his sister that the fish she'd served him was pretty small. She snatched the fish from his plate and slapped him hard across the face with it. It was left to Walter some weeks later to go around to his uncle's apartment and persuade him to come to Walter's Bar Mitzvah.

"You know, I didn't like my mother very much," he remarked to me recently at breakfast in Rio. Just before the coronavirus. At ninety-seven. It was the first time I had heard him say such a thing.

Just before the war broke out, his father ordered him back to England from Switzerland, where he'd been sent to another boarding school in Lausanne after the Billinghurst episode. His father ordered him to take the train.

Set some time during the war years in London is another of his rare anecdotes. I have not reminded him of this story in the last fifty-five years. He told me that walking the streets as a teenager in London he was required to wear a helmet. One day shrapnel hit the helmet and knocked him down. He told me the helmet had saved his life. At my prodding, he told me this story in Brazil several times; I was thirteen, fourteen.

His vocabulary in English is excellent, better than Portuguese. His accent, near neutral, retains faint echoes of his British years. He has a few specialized terms. Those who died in the Holocaust are unfailingly referred to as having "perished."

He was and is the most secretive person I have met. He is as discreet, modulated, and restrained in his dress as in his demeanour. In the sixty-five years I have known him I have never seen him naked. He claims that he has never dreamed.

Shortly after his return from Lausanne to London, Senhor Valter and his parents emigrated to Canada and settled in Montreal. They travelled in a convoy across the North Atlantic, evading the U-boats.

He was twenty-one when he arrived in Montreal in the early forties: what did he find there?

From the man-made mist lingering over these years emerge four figures, two couples who became friendly. Three Montrealers born and bred, and Senhor Valter, recently arrived from Prostějov, Zagreb, London, and Lausanne, arriving after that weeks-long voyage across the North Atlantic. In Montreal his first name change occurred, this one official, from Gunsberg to Gainsbury.

In their first configuration, these four figures emerge in the mist as Walter Gainsbury and Judith Gainsbury (née Judith Sorel Riven), who marry in Montreal and become parents in the later forties to two boys, Lawrence and Philip; and Mortimer Besner and Judith Besner (née Judith Francis Cohen), who marry in Montreal and become parents in the later forties to two boys, Derek and Neil.

Before the four boys are born, these couples are friendly in that misty mid-forties Montreal. Before, during — and after?

It is here that storytelling becomes confounded.

Story, fairy tale, memory, dream. It depends on the season. It depends on time and on place. In Brazil, in the early sixties, there are only the stories told by Senhor Valter and his wife, Dona Judite, two of those four fast friends from mid-forties Montreal. Derek and Neil, who arrived in Brazil with Senhor Valter and Dona Judite in September 1956, know these few stories by heart, but the stories never cohere.

Senhor Valter has never believed in breakdowns, but he was immobilized once, when his youngest son Michael, born in Montreal to Dona Judite in 1958, the first of their two children in his second marriage in Montreal, June 1956, died in a car accident in Rio in August 1983. Dona Judite had returned to Montreal from Rio to give birth to her son in Canada; or had she returned because she had left Senhor Valter? It is not known. The stories vary.

But for a time, in August 1983, the contours of the formally casual posture Senhor Valter had studied for life became more accented, the creases in his slacks more exact than ever, his pale green sports shirts, opened past the second button, revealing this terrible trouble, which he bore four-square.

He would sit then, legs carefully crossed, in the captain's chair by the pool at the front of the big house in Leblon at 549 Rua Codajás, the house that he had built to exacting specifications, his and Dona Judite's, in the later sixties in Rio de Janeiro. He should have been in his office downtown by now, but he couldn't bring himself to go to work. He tested the tip of a toothpick against a fingertip. The circumference of his activities was narrowed to the captain's chair. All of his authority, the sweep and the range and the scope of his powers concentrated themselves into this immobility.

But let us return to the mid-fifties, when Senhor Valter moved to Brazil with his new family, with Judith Francis née Cohen, formerly Judith Besner, soon to become Dona

Judite, and her two sons from her first marriage, the two little boys, Derek and Neil. This is when Senhor Valter acquired his Brazilian name and began to acquire his fortune. He was naturalized in Brazil in the mid-seventies.

Naturalized is the term, but there is no naturalizing Senhor Valter.

Senhor Valter is a citizen of his own cosmopolis, with allegiance to no country save the Empire of Reason. Which, he proclaimed to my older brother Derek and me at the dinner table when we were young teenagers in Rio, could resolve anything. His favourite word in English? "Absolutely." Did he love us? Absolutely he did, he does.

In the mid-fifties he brought a textile mill from Quebec to Rio de Janeiro, then sold it at great profit. Why did he leave Montreal and move to South America? Stories vary. It is not known. He lost a large sum of money in a failed clothing business, runs one version. In another, there was no clothing business. What brought him to Rio de Janeiro with his textile mill? It remains unknown.

In the next thirty years in Brazil, he became wealthy, and he became generous with his wealth. A shipping company, a bookstore; a large pineapple plantation in the north of the country. But in 1983, the death of his last-born son immobilized him for a time, and a few years later, rising business troubles began to lap at the foundations of his empire. By the early nineties, the empire had begun its collapse. By the mid-nineties, it was gone.

Senhor Valter's carefully modulated control began to

slip soon after; his temper, so long beautifully controlled, began to get the better of him. He became impetuous. He began to yell at his partner Rochelle, who, by the late 1970s, had succeeded Dona Judite in Brazil in public.

I asked Rochelle in 2012 why she now put up with Senhor Valter's temper. She said, "I tell myself that he lost a son and he lost a fortune."

Memory's confidences, quotations from memory, are not to be trusted. But neither is the lockstep arrogance of chronology. Who can apprehend the passing of time? Is memory a loom that shuttles and weaves across chronology? Returning, wilfully and skilfully, unerringly and relentlessly to imagined beginnings?

No. And the fat adverbs only provoke and incite.

Ironically, Michael's death had what might from others' callow points of view have been seen as a salutary effect on Senhor Valter. He had long been famed for arriving, casually, notoriously late, sometimes hours late, for social occasions — dinners, gatherings. He shrugged off complaints; this obsession with trivial punctuality was a sign, he advised, of neurotic insecurity. Of a thin and unattractive need to be loved.

Immediately following the loss of his son and permanently thereafter, however, Senhor Valter became obsessively punctual. More, on the eve of any departure, he called several members of the family to advise them, precisely, of his travel itinerary, departures and arrivals via which airline, what flight number. He advised of arrangements to rent a car, with which company, at what rate. He advised, precisely, of delays en route. *In real time*, as they say.

Each in his own wrong way, Senhor Valter and I have tried, for nearly all my life and for well over half of his, by routes consistently, faithfully chosen to ensure their failure to reach their destination, to approach each other. When I reached twenty, things exploded.

From Senhor Valter's point of view, this change constituted a hurtful betrayal.

When I was fifteen, a month before embarking on the *Ponta Negra*, I offered to help Senhor Valter with the text of a pamphlet he had just designed to promote his Brazilian shipping company's imminent expansion from its coastal range in South America to a hard-won transatlantic reach, Boston, New York, Montreal. He was delighted with me. He gave me several of his Marlboros as I worked at the draft pamphlet in the Winter Garden of our small rented house at 126 Codajás. The Marlboros were smooth, American, filtered. These were unlike Tardelli's stubby Brazilian Continentals; unlike Tardelli's matchboxes, Senhor Valter's elegant thin gold-plated lighter sat by my side at the table. At the end of an hour and a half, I suggested perhaps twelve revisions in ten pages of text.

He thanked me profusely. He was grateful for his precocious stepson's interest, the one who had inherited a flair with words from his mother, herself a famed letter writer. Then he reviewed the pamphlet with me, explaining, carefully, slowly, precisely — reasonably; painstakingly — how and why each one, every one of my suggestions was wrong. Why the original was preferable. And reinstalled. He thanked me profusely once again for my interest.

When I remind him over the years, jocularly, of this episode, he grins cheerfully, shakes his head, marvelling, and admits he has no memory of it. He remembers the Winter Garden in the small rented house, the Marlboros — he stopped smoking many years ago. He remembers his gold-plated lighter, he remembers the pamphlet. (I have the pamphlet.) But not this episode.

It is not simple, our mutual détente. I am more responsible for its cool immobility than is Senhor Valter. When he tried to teach me — and he knew, he knows many things that surprise me — I became mulish, distracted, silent. Politely hostile.

That same summer, June 1965, we took a boat trip with Tardelli on Senhor Valter's 29-foot cruiser, from Rio to Angra dos Reis, a little community five hours south, down the coast. Derek and Philip came with us. To Tardelli's amusement they got seasick on the way back. Puking out of opposite sides of the boat. "Pintando a lancha," he winked at me. Painting the boat. Senhor Valter laughed.

On the way to Angra, he beckoned me below, to a table with a map and a compass. He wished to show me how to navigate, how to plot a route, calculate distance, speed, to estimate hours. I had no idea that he knew how to navigate. He showed me, motioning me to bend over the map with him, our heads close together, as he deftly manipulated the two points of the compass across the map, crossing one point with precision over the other, tracing our route. Explaining carefully, precisely, what he was doing. He wished to instruct me.

All that I sensed at that moment, and most of what I remember, is the faintly stale but strong smell of coffee on his breath. Very little of what he said, of what he showed me, remains.

I have reflected for fifty-five years on the import of this moment. It has become juxtaposed with the pamphlet incident. It is entirely of my making, this wilfulness; it is entirely in character. Alongside each other, Senhor Valter on his route, me on mine.

Grievance, blame, do not enter this equation. The episodes constitute a chapter in the Samizdat sensation *Stepfathers and Stepsons*. It has always been unfair of me to demand that he be different, that he be my father. Or that he be like Tardelli.

But fairness has nothing to do with it. I love him far more than I like him, but it is forced love, love that began at five, love that exploded, that was dynamited by the time I was twenty. Not because Senhor Valter had changed, but because I had.

Senhor Valter rescued us, the little boys, Derek and Neil, from a dark apartment on Sherbrooke Street. He brought light and reason, sunshine and calm. He brought predictability. He soothed Dona Judite's meteoric passions. He saved us. This is what I saw, until I didn't.

He took a friendly interest in my fishing with Tardelli. He told me it was a healthy life, until it wasn't.

When I was fourteen, I persuaded him to come fishing with us. I persuaded him to take the bus with me to the yacht club on a Sunday and to take his second boat, the *Judite*, named after my mother. We embarked, Tardelli, Senhor Valter, and me. This was confusing. Senhor Valter wore a blue bathing suit — the wrong thing to wear. Tardelli wore his official whites, the wrong things to wear. Tardelli didn't sing opera, as was his custom.

We went to Ilha do Pai, Father's Island, a few miles from the mouth of the bay, and on the southern point, we caught five small bluefish. I have a photograph of Senhor Valter from this first outing, standing at the stern, fumbling with the line. Tardelli taught him how to handline. Looking at his clumsiness, his fumbling with the line snarled at his feet, I am ashamed to admit that I felt superior. More evidence, like the absurd blue bathing suit, that all of this was foreign to him, while I played the knowing native. Tardelli's ally, his son.

When we returned to the yacht club Senhor Valter was happy, enthused. Delighted. I was happy as well. Tardelli murmured to him, and he slipped Tardelli some small bills as per habit.

Thus began Senhor Valter's fishing. It progressed from bluefish — we went out five or six times — to marlin, dorado, to teams and international tournaments. The boats got bigger. By this time I was in my twenties and I had left the old routine of fishing with Tardelli for bluefish. I returned to Brazil only sporadically. Tardelli complained to me quietly about Senhor Valter's Brazilian team, a demanding bunch who yelled at Tardelli.

I could not and cannot demand that Senhor Valter be someone else. He has tried all his life, by his lights, to be my father. He has tried, all his life, to gaze, more than benign, upon my interests.

I took up guitar when I was twelve. My mother took me to Anton Wilfer's guitar shop on Mackay Street in Montreal and bought me my first instrument. It was to compensate, she told me, for all the attention being paid to my older brother Derek in his Bar Mitzvah year. Back in Brazil, I flayed at it with a broken-off clothespin until I was given lessons. A few months later, Senhor Valter paused outside the screen door of the Winter Garden, early afternoon, a weekend day. "Play every song you know," he said to me, kindly, then stood there silently for twenty minutes as I did.

Last year, at his and Rochelle's request, I took my new Martin to their condo and played for them. It was an occasion. Their cook recorded me. Rochelle asked me how I had learned to sing in my "cowboy voice." Senhor Valter beamed, silent.

By his lights, he loved me then, he loves me now. We do not like each other. I love him, but love is a difficult word and an even more difficult feeling. That Senhor Valter and I intend something entirely different by the word does not assist in conferring the feeling upon either of us.

No matter how far back I recede, none of the love stories endure. They will not still themselves. They swirl, they migrate, from the mid-sixties, at the mouth of the bay, Boca da Barra, back to Montreal, to the misty era before that first fabled arrival in Brazil by ship, September 1956. Irregular memory's sudden lightning, like its sisterly swimming in southern oceans, is unpredictable but always imminent, as close to immanent as memory can be.

I have, unreasonably, required memory to do so much work. To stand as sole keeper of the sacred, the spiritual, and the divine, now that these powers have gone out from the world.

Dona Judite told the three of us at dinner one evening in the early sixties, at a favoured Chinese restaurant in Leblon, ten minutes' walk away from our first small rented house, that old sense of mystery had vanished. She was reflective, regretful, but matter of fact. The four of us at the table, Senhor Valter, Dona Judite, the two young teenaged boys, fell quiet. The parents smoked their cigarettes, her Salem, his Marlboro. A momentary calm descended over the ginger beef and the rice. Communal loss.

Memory is first cousin to lateral association; they animate connected, echoing compartments in Proust's cork-lined chambers. What is the relation between memory and the imagination, Marcel? You spend over three thousand pages asking, and you reach an answer that serves your exalted purpose. It is not because I read it in translation that I came away with no answer like yours, save for an insisting thudding, a clamour in my chest.

The SS *Argentina* eased shoreward on a warm September morning in 1956. *Why*, I used to wonder as a little boy, *did we come to Brazil on a ship named the* SS Argentina*?* She rubs against the dock in the port in Rio; we boys lean out over the railing and watch sailors hauling up thick-ribbed yellow ropes. Coming down the gangplank an hour later, Derek looks over at one of the ropes, his eye caught by the movement of a large rat on its way aboard. It sways, fat and grey and ungainly. He tells no one, keeping the image and later the memory to himself.

It was the first of many secrets: a rat, grey and ungainly, crawling up the thick looping rope on a hazy morning that smelled of oil in the heat. When he remembers the rat, he also remembers hearing his first Portuguese word — rato — sounding like waves would if they weren't water, when the world began to shimmer.

Maybe Derek once felt the need, each time he summoned up that memory, to learn, quickly, how to tread water in order to stay afloat. I don't really know. I don't know what he remembers. I don't know how he felt. I don't know if he saw that rat. I did. This isn't a novel.

I do know that the summer I boarded the *Ponta Negra*, one grey June day in 1965, walking along the beach in Leblon on my way home from fishing with Tardelli — I'd gotten off the bus early — I spotted Derek a hundred metres away, walking towards me. This was odd. That was the era when Derek spent much of his time alone in his room, gripped by something sombre and silent. To run into him in the world, here on the beach, was more than unlikely. We exchanged brief rueful words, a rueful recognition. Went our ways. I chugged a large bottle of very cold beer at a corner botequim, a bar — there was one on most corners on Ataulfo de Paiva, the main street, two blocks in from the beach — before getting home.

Is this a fairy tale, then? Or something from the Bible?

For lo, let us hearken back to mid-forties Montreal, in that once upon a time, when the two Judiths and their first spouses form a warm Jewish quartet. This long-ago foursome dances through the gay Montreal of the time, stopping in at the Ritz Carlton, its cheery red-faced liveried doormen (Jimmy and his compeers) known by name to all. The foursome has a drink at the Mount Royal Hotel; they gather at downtown gambling emporia owned by dashing Jewish gangsters, fleeing, the lore has it, from crimes in

America, in Chicago, Detroit — like Max Shapiro, who later comes to own Ruby Foo's, the Chinese restaurant long favoured by the Montreal Jewish community. Fedoras set at jaunty angles. Maroon sedans sliding alongside the streetcars trundling down Sherbrooke Street. Sainte-Catherine not yet overtaken by today's throngs in carefully torn jeans.

Not the Bible. No, in one of its modes, this is a love story, Senhor Valter's and Dona Judite's.

Well then, a love story that begins in a biblical place: Eden, before the expulsion. Yea, and rising up from Sherbrooke Street on its southern brow, there tower the silent and stern and grandiloquent hills of upper Westmount, fabled and fabulous. Those lofty snowy hills and sinuous sidehills descend in summer to the leafy plains of Sherbrooke Street — lined, those hills, with the quarried and pedigreed stone-faced homes that peered and still do peer down in mild and muted disapproval onto Sherbrooke Street's or, on another of Mount Royal's brows, Queen Mary's stolid brownstones, stalwart edifices of sound if lesser repute.

It is from these, from those imagined heights, I later reflect, that my maternal grandmother Jennie Cohen, née Jennie Heillig, sometimes in the kitchen, sometimes in the breakfast room in her house on the southeast corner of Argyle, 4332 Westmount Avenue, would pronounce mysteriously, sombrely, shaking her head, her repeated cryptic phrases: "Those two. The irresponsibility." It took me years, first to understand to whom she was referring — "Those two" — and then years more to apprehend the significance of the pronouncement.

To remember, then to imagine? No. These are not chronological nor sequential, nor causally related activities. Nor are they activities.

It's there, if you believe in thereness; then, if you believe in then; or, lo, beginning, as if once upon a time, or in the Bible, or in the mid-1940s, that Senhor Valter's and Dona Judite's love story began, begins.

But this is also when names begin to echo, to repeat and then resonate as if they signified, as if this were a fiction, on its way, over cobblestones, to a fable.

A delicious word for cobblestones in Portuguese: paralelépipedo. Portuguese: the American kids Derek and I knew in Brazil in the late fifties sneered, called it "Pork and Cheese." We looked down on these barbarians, their crew socks in their American running shoes, their arrogance and their buzz cuts and their American bubble gum.

Portuguese: as I myself grew, unknowingly, increasingly defensive against interiority, I began with desperate intent to play amid languages as a shield. By the time I was at university in North America, and we were taught about the Greek meeting place, the Agora, I had taught myself to slip sidelong into Portuguese — agora, now — so that my childhood dreaminess, much castigated by Senhor Valter and Dona Judite, now became the frenetic unease of my twenties, abetting this translation of my mounting

45

agoraphobia via wordplay: fear of the now, agora, conflating the panic at being out in the open with the fear of presence, of being suddenly marooned, somewhere, anywhere in the present. Here, now: a bilingual fear of the here and now. *Agora*phobia.

This recourse to words as bilingual battlements drove me in turn to study and then to teach literature. I spent decades caught suddenly breathless in the present, standing in front of a group at the beginning of each class, fighting off the urge to break and run. Unknowing, I fastened, desperate, onto novels and poems about time redeemed. I wrote a master's thesis on Saul Bellow, departed from Lachine at an early age for Chicago; a Ph.D. on Mavis Gallant, who left Montreal for Europe in her twenties. I discovered these parallel biographical currents in my late thirties.

I taught Atwood's "There is only one of everything" everywhere, in and out of class. To groups of Winnipeg businessmen. At United Way cabinet meetings.

I paused endlessly on Atwood's closing lines:

> . . . I can even
> say it, though only once and it won't
> last: I want this. I want
> this.

She says it twice, after promising she'll only say it once. As time passes in us, time present, and this, and this, and this. Saved, for a time, by love. By this. At least, she is, for a time.

But words haven't been enough. To this day I cannot walk out onto Senhor Valter's balcony high up over the beach. I remain, already anxious and dizzying, in the living room. If he goes out onto the balcony, we converse through the screen door. Warm summer evenings, Senhor Valter, flawless in his generosity, arranges for the dining room table to be placed one quarter inside, the rest of the company out on the balcony; I sit, an honoured guest, at the head, inside, agoraphobia become vertical, translated up and down.

Whose fault is it that I cannot stay with him at his condo, cannot walk out onto his balcony with him? It is no one's fault. There is no remedy. The remedy is, don't stay at the condo. Don't go out onto the balcony. Don't walk over bridges.

Remember: before they become Senhor Valter and Dona Judite in Brazil, they are Walter Gainsbury (née Gunsberg) and Judith Besner (née Cohen) of Montreal, and they are married to others. As I have related. Before I am born, they meet each other. But first, they are married to others.

And lo, the two Founding Mothers of these soon-to-be commingled families were both Judith yclept. The Founding Fathers, out of respect, perhaps, for the coincident Judiths, surrendered their customary appellations for a half-century and came to be known to their respective sons, two migrated from each Founding Family, as Unca (Senhor Valter) and as Par. Until, late in the twentieth century, the four sons, now adults, resurrected their father's names and they became, once again, twin familiars: "Dad."

But here, some five years before I was born, memory cannot tell time. It is not because I wasn't alive, but because these four had no reliable memories of mid-forties Montreal that they wish to vouchsafe to any of their first four children. They did not wish to say. What little that has been narrated remains contradictory. The stories don't add up.

In Brazil, in the early sixties, as I have related, there are only the stories of Senhor Valter and his wife, Dona Judite, two of those four fast friends from Montreal.

When Senhor Valter and Dona Judite speak of Montreal in the mid-sixties, in Brazil, it is in passing. It is brief, dismissive. "That provincial backwater," offers Dona Judite more than once at dinner. Senhor Valter concurs by saying nothing; his circumspection is eloquent. We two boys, now young teenagers, are rapt but wary.

The four little boys from those two original marriages in Montreal in the mid- to late-forties, Derek and Neil, Lawrence and Philip, first met over ginger ale in bottles, proffered on a Sunday, mid-afternoon, August 1956, in my mother's Montreal apartment on Sherbrooke Street. Before she became Dona Judite in Brazil. Strange shade inside, bright sunlight outside.

In that Sherbrooke Street apartment — now it is in the Chateau Redfern, but then the building was nameless. Now it has been sandblasted; then it was, the story goes, owned by my father's father, J.A. Besner, a.k.a., on the Main, The Judge. Before acquiring his Brazilian name, Senhor Valter lay asleep with my mother in her bedroom when I was awakened one summer night by the bang of thunder. I ran into her room; he took me into bed, cradled my head under his arm. It was uncomfortable, a hard arm. Next morning he cheerfully swept up spilled Rice Krispies in the kitchen. A revelation, this lightness.

Years later, this became another paradox, unresolvable. Senhor Valter brought calm, reason, laughter, an unremitting cheer into our dark apartment. But how, then, did he suddenly appear? And then, more subtly, over decades, disappear?

Below that third-floor Sherbrooke Street apartment there was, there is, a little island of a park across the street. Derek and I are on tricycles with my father on one of his visits. My mother is close by. The sky is dark and still with approaching rain. A rumble of thunder; the world pauses. The adults glance at the sky and then meaningfully at each other. We are hurried inside before the storm breaks. That stillness, that breathless pause, sits with me.

I climb the fire escape up the back of the building with the janitor's son and we get to the roof, triumphant. My mother is told. She calls my father. "If you don't spank him I will," I hear. He arrives from somewhere in the city, pats me gently five, six times over his knee. My mother does not intervene. He's gone.

Out the back window of the apartment, I throw the new short-legged suits my mother has outfitted us with, custom-made, princely clothes made at her father's clothing company. I cannot remember the consequence of this act.

This is not, as I have said, a novel. Nor are there world-views or morals to be inferred.

In the early fall of 1956, the first day of the new school year, I was told by my first-grade teacher in Montreal that we would be moving to Brazil. That evening, sitting with my mother in the kitchen in the Sherbrooke Street apartment, my older brother Derek and I learned that in Brazil we were going to have to drink bottled water. We were not to drink from the taps, we could get typhoid. Often, late at night in our apartment in Copacabana, more truly thirsty than truly frightened, I did, and survived. In that early era in Brazil, I would awaken each night for several weeks and look at the small and ominous helicopter that had, somehow, landed in our bedroom in the dark, and was poised, motionless but menacing, on a chair a few feet from my bed, and I was afraid.

It was in those years that Walter — before he became Senhor Valter, not to be gainsaid — began to decree his bedrock if unarticulated belief, his unpronounced sine qua non, that we suddenly became one large and happy family. North and south. A belief in place of anyone's memory, including his own.

But memory will persist in weaving other stories.

What story led from the mid-forties to the mid-fifties?

In one enduring form, it remains their love story.

Or, it was my mother's story, alluding, darkly, to my father's gambling addiction. *That* was the wedge. Senhor Valter was either silent or allowed that in those years my mother was pursued by "half of Montreal." Which made him the victor.

My father never said a word to anyone. He had no story to tell. He did tell me several times, when I was in my early twenties, of the six months he had spent living with his parents in their house on Elm Avenue (pronounced in his generation as *Ellum* Avenue) at one unidentified time in his adult life. He told me he hadn't wanted to leave the house. It took me decades to understand his Morse Code, to understand that he had retreated from the world when he was left.

There were other stories from the mid- to late-forties. One recounted a note on a windshield on Sherbrooke Street, advising the wronged Judith that her husband was at that moment in a nearby hotel room with the other Judith.

None of these accounts stood up. All of them stood up.

In one telling, it is their love story. I have laboured but failed to apprehend it from the real love letters they wrote each other, sequestered by Dona Judite in Rio in an old worn blue suitcase I discovered in her condo there a year before she died in 2003. I have further assembled the love story from a black and white photograph that I stole then from that suitcase, of Senhor Valter and Dona Judite at a rooftop restaurant in Montreal, named and dated on the back in blue ink, in my mother's immaculately regular handwriting: *The Normandie Roof, May 1944.* Before their marriages to others.

In the photo he is gazing at her; she is looking at the camera. He is wearing a dark suit, wide lapels, wide pinstripe. The beginning of a hopeful smile plays at his lips. Looking at the camera, she is radiant. She would have been nineteen but she looks twenty-two, twenty-three. She is wearing a print dinner dress, pearls at her neck. Both have a drink in front of them. It looks like a martini. Senhor Valter stopped drinking abruptly, permanently, in the early fifties. As he stopped smoking, abruptly, permanently, in the late seventies. His mantra: *Willpower. Reason.*

In the hundreds of letters in the suitcase, hers handwritten, his typed, they called each other, repeatedly, *Pussycat*, but no one has heard them say that word to each other in daylight.

For many years, I wondered whether Senhor Valter was, in fact, my father. In 2005, in Rio, I asked him that, during a casual conversation at lunch, at a churrascaria, with Rochelle. Dona Judite had been gone for two years. He hesitated, smiling, calculating the years. I explained that a simple DNA test could quickly tell us. He became very pleased at the prospect. Another son, to replace the sparring, bantering stepson.

In the weeks that passed before we got the results, I agonized. I would have to reconceive of myself entirely, my history, my health, my past, my feelings. My behaviour. My relationship with Europe and with Senhor Valter. With the biologies, the psychologies, the degrees of relation with my brothers and sisters, whom I would have to imagine differently.

The test, shuttled back and forth between Rio, Winnipeg, and an American lab, came back negative. Senhor Valter was disappointed.

"Look Neil, either you're sick or you're not sick," Senhor Valter said to me. I was twenty-one, standing with him in my mother's parents' kitchen in Montreal, at 4332, which Derek and I had dubbed the Ponderosa. It was a few months after the long-distance call from Rio to LA, *Drop the aggression, Neil.* "Drop," cut short, carried his European intonation, his impeccably learned English.

I am told Senhor Valter sat down some weeks after that in Montreal with Dr. Katz, a psychiatrist. Asked him, "Well, Doctor, any brain damage?"

You upset him, you old Charmer. Quoting Senhor Valter to me, Dr. Katz told me he'd risen out of his chair in anger. A few days later Senhor Valter told me, yes, that was indeed what Dr. Katz had done. Senhor Valter told me that he then instructed Dr. Katz, calmly, to sit down, and then Senhor Valter told him what's what.

It helps no one to dwell on, to recount these little hurts. In Saul Bellow's novel *Henderson the Rain King* — a repository of quotable lines, gorgeous insights tossed off or dressed up in madcap characters' pronouncements — Joni Mitchell, an avid Bellow reader, lifts lines from near the end of the novel to sing to us that she's "looked at clouds from both sides now" — a magnificent African King Dhafu tries to teach Henderson that he must "hold the blow," that he must learn to not act on his manifold grievances, or narrate them, or pass on his wounds to others. He must hold them to himself. And this is what humanity must do.

Sadly, King Dhafu comes to a bad end. But his sentiment — not that Henderson learns to act on it — resonates. Although Henderson also remarks: "I am to suffering what Gary, Indiana, is to smoke — the word's biggest operation."

We must hold the blow. In this Senhor Valter has been more successful than I have been.

The four little boys, Derek and Neil, Lawrence and Philip, grew up and married in the seventies. My lifelong fascination with happenstance and the slant resonance of recurring names and their variations, begun with the two Judies, grew after I married last: our wives in chronological order were Helene, Elaine, Eileen, and Carlene. None knew each other, none were from the same place or were married in the same place.

My father, still Par then, was nonplussed. Eventually, he took to referring to them all as "Dear." Unca, Walter Gunsberg, Walter Gainsbury, Senhor Valter, Dad, remembers each of the women's names precisely to this day.

Some of our marriages ended; two second wives bore the burdens of the names of two of the children from our first marriages, Jennifer, Barbara. By the time Walter, Senhor Valter, and my mother, his second Judy, Dona Judite, had dissolved in Brazil in the later 1970s and he had emerged in public with Rochelle, it seemed only natural, although not by design, that his new partner bore the same name as his second child and only daughter by his second marriage, his Brazilian-born daughter Jo-Anne's middle name.

Names, first words, and happenstance: maybe that's why I do not accept distinctions between stories and so-called real life. Between memoir and story. Why I have conducted a lifelong affair with words and a more complicated affair with memory and time. So that the past has always shimmered too close to *once upon a time*.

From very early on, memory became the most sinuous storyteller of all. Washing away the statistical infirmities, chronology, month and year, age.

Let us return, then, to one beginning, in Rio, mid-summer, Brazilian winter, July 1965, when, as I was saying, I was put aboard, when I boarded the *Ponta Negra*. I had misbehaved; I had gotten drunk on my own boat, a 21-foot lapstrake, a prototype made by famed Brazilian boat manu-facturer Carbrasmar. Powered by an inboard Ford F-150 truck motor.

I had "lost my dignity," intoned Senhor Valter. I had endangered the two girls with me, my age, schoolmates several years earlier from the British School of Rio, 76 Rua da Matriz in Botafogo. Can I name them? Of course I can name them, and one's older brother, the other's older sister.

> The British School of Rio
> has blazoned on its crest
> Our motto Semper Optimum
> We always do our best.

I had become blind drunk on rum and desire. Tardelli and others fumbled me into a shower and then into a taxi home, a twenty-minute ride to Leblon. Two of my brothers — rather, Derek and my stepbrother Philip, living with us in Brazil that summer — hid me, half-conscious, singing lewd lyrics in Portuguese, they told me later, in the garage beneath the house, but Floriana the cook, one of Tardelli's lovers, as I have said, ratted me out the next day.

The day before I boarded the *Ponta Negra*, I walked up to a store that sold fishing tackle on Ataulfo de Paiva, the main street in Leblon, fifteen minutes from the house. I bought unpainted lead lures, feathers, hooks, a spool of thin wire to wrap and clamp around the hook, and another plastic spool of thick nylon line.

The morning I left the house for the *Ponta Negra*, my mother, Dona Judite, formally dressed in a skirt printed as a Scots kilt, said "take care of yourself" to me. Stern, nervous, terse. Subdued. Standing in the living room encircled by the sterile silence begot by the mentholated fumes from her Salems.

What was she feeling? What had passed between her and Senhor Valter? I felt defiant. I felt I had won a battle in an undeclared war.

She is always there in her stylish kilt; there she is. Who knew her? She was widely admired, more widely unknown. There she is, Dona Judite in those years, an inverse Mrs. Dalloway before one of her legendary parties, gathering herself in our small back yard in the small rented house in

Leblon, sitting beneath the lime tree with her Scotch in a small crystal tumbler, a Salem in her other hand.

"So you lost your cherry," she said to me when Senhor Valter brought me back to the house that late August.

"What an experience!" he marvelled in the car on the way home. He meant something else.

The *Ponta Negra* moved out past the old fort at the Boca da Barra. She was 1650 tons with a crew of twelve. She sailed south in mid-July 1965 from Rio to Santos, the port for the city of São Paulo, and loaded coffee and some deck cargo, including a bright red jeep, then sailed to Salvador, Bahia, docked for one day, and sailed again for twelve days to Belém and the mouth of the Amazon. Supervising the improvised unloading of the jeep in Manaus, watching as it dangled and swayed twenty feet up, caused florid Sebastião, the company agent, to redden further and to lose his temper and yell at the crew. Not able to abide the death of his father years later, I learned, Sebastião shot himself with a rifle.

There were long rocking days out of sight of the coast. There was a gnarled wooden pole strung aft with two braided lines, trawling for marlin, dorado. There was the alternately darker blue and brighter blue and white-foaming sea and the circling sun. One evening one of the sailors shrugged and said to me that it probably wasn't a good idea to sit on the stern like that, too easy to fall back into the ship's wake. I got down and lit a cigarette; in 1965 this was still an unfiltered Brazilian Continental, held between the thumb and forefinger. I flicked the ash away, ruminative, like Tardelli, with the third or fourth finger.

Why did I need to love him so much?

At Belém, near the mouth of the Amazon, the *Ponta Negra* took on two river pilots, Zé Maria and Esmeraldino. *Zé* is short for *José*, Joseph. Esmeraldino had been a body-guard for President Juscelino Kubitschek, progenitor of Brasília. Both men were talkative and river smart. For indiscernible reasons both were armed. Before heading upriver the *Ponta Negra* met the *Praia Grande*, her sister ship, in Belém and lay at dock for two days. The two captains drank beer at a small table set up at the stern of the *Praia Grande*. A dark-haired woman with green eyes lounged with them. There was music from a transistor radio. They smoked cigars and drank beer; they played a desultory card game in the heat.

The captain of the *Ponta Negra*, Comandante José Serra, was at twenty-eight the youngest at his rank in the Brazilian coastal merchant marine; the captain of the *Praia Grande*, his friend Cesário, was in his forties. Of the crew of the *Ponta Negra*, those who remain in memory's pantomime include Manecão the cook (big Mané), his assistant Manequinho (little Mané), and the bespectacled chief engineer Senhor João Vitoria, with his pipe and a resonant voice for a small man. He was the proprietor of a silent oncinha, a young wildcat with intense green eyes that lived in the top drawer of his dresser. You could stroke her if you were gentle and didn't touch her head.

Two days out of Santos, heading north up the coast towards Belém, Manequinho knocks at my window to wake me. The water from my showerhead, improperly shut down, has flooded my room and is now issuing onto the deck. Laughing, he doesn't let me forget this for days, but he tells no one else.

The first mate is Juarez, black hair and a gold tooth, whistled at and beckoned by the women in bars in every port. At sea he teaches me rope knots like the mão de amigo, friend's hand. Indio is named for his origins somewhere in Amazonas. Pará, bright blue eyes, is named for his home state. Young Adão the telegraph operator, nimble-fingered at Morse Code, is very good at futebol, soccer, on the small river beaches.

Ahmed, the second mate, is a tall and balding Arab on his maiden voyage on the *Ponta Negra* who goes pale with seasickness out of Rio the first night — "balanço chato, não é?" — annoying pitching, isn't it? — but revives. Weeks later on the Amazon, in Manaus, he entertains two girls with me, Aria and Nazaré, in his bunkroom. This is after my night with Minose, who comes with me from the bar where we've danced to accordion music and bumps in a taxi down a dark dirt road back to the ship.

In my bunk, she smells faintly of a watery perfume. Brown body, darker brown nipples. She wants it from behind. She looks at me throbbing, and giggles. As we're finishing, she shakes beneath me, hugs me to her back, curls me to her tightly and falls asleep.

I awoke again soon, but she was fast asleep and I was too shy to wake her. In the morning she was gone.

Fifty-five years later I can hear her giggling, and I can see her dancing high-hipped in jeans and a white top. The bar is strung with hanging loops of coloured light bulbs. I can hear her in bed, telling me to look her in the eyes — "assim não presta," like that is no good, she told me when I tried to look away.

A week earlier in Santarém, I first lay with and then lied to a young woman. I told her I was an assistant to the engineer. To myself I lied otherwise, in English, *So that's all it is?*

On the way to Manaus the *Ponta Negra* stopped in several small river ports. In my thirties and forties I believed I would never forget the order of this progress, but I have forgotten it. Only the names remain: Óbidos, Itacoatiara, Parintins, Oriximiná. Of course Santarém.

An hour out of Itacoatiara, a hot afternoon, the *Ponta Negra* stills to a drift midriver and blows one steam-filled blast on her whistle. A long canoe appears alongside. Two crewmen pass down a large canvas sack of rice, another of black beans. There are three Indians in the canoe; in exchange they hoist up a catfish as long and as thick as a man.

No photographs of this prearranged meeting remain. I did take one of the catfish, but it has vanished. Two men and a woman, the three wore no clothing and there was not much else in the canoe. In memory, they have an indistinct dark colour. They are smiling, they are speaking, not in Portuguese. The two crewmen understand them. The episode unfolds in minutes. The colour of the Amazon here is a rich and amplifying brown, carrying itself wide, and wide, to an indistinct far bank.

The next day we pass through the Estreito de Boaçu, the Strait of Boaçu. Now I cannot find it on a map. It seems as if you could touch both banks. The two river pilots, both alert and upright in the wheelhouse, call out terse commands. The water is darker, the bright green parrots are raucous and scolding everywhere. We emerge again into the broad brown river, flat to its far, far bank.

In Manaus, fishing off the ship with a handline baited with cheese, I saw a young girl in a canoe who came by the *Ponta Negra* every afternoon for six days on her way to somewhere forever undiscovered. On the second day in port, someone aboard christened her Maria das Canoas — Mary of the Canoes. She liked that. She smiled up at us every afternoon after. Like her new name, her smile remains.

No one in 1965 on the *Ponta Negra* or on land mentioned the Opera House in Manaus, although one could see its gorgeous blue dome clearly from on deck. The crew, dry at sea, now drank volubly in port. No one on board, nor I, had heard of the poet Elizabeth Bishop. In my fifties I discovered Bishop's great, late poem, "Santarém," and wrote about it, but this did not help very much. I thought I understood the first lines:

> Of course I may be remembering it all wrong
> after, after — how many years?

But I didn't. For years I was only capable of reading these lines literally: "remembering it all wrong," I believed, could only signify that there was a right way, a right memory. A true memory. Other memories were simply made up. They were stories. I was "starving in some deep mystery / Like a man who is sure what is true," as the early Cohen drones. I still am. Driving around LA at eighteen, lost, I remember looking at my arm, thinking, this is who I am, this is myself. My Self.

A psychologist in Winnipeg said to me, in my forties, "Your categories are primitive." Driving around LA, I knew myself as the proprietor of the arm on the steering wheel. Except that sudden rages erupted at two in the morning, driving me to a notebook, wherein I recorded, "Fucking switchies they pulled on me!"

So much for holding the blow.

Looking back now I see that we were out of reach of history in Brazil, including the more haunting and dangerous reach of my father and his new family in Montreal. In the early sixties jet planes had recently come into service, having replaced the three-tailed constellation, the Super G on which we descended once to Brazil in the late fifties. But mere developments in mechanical speed couldn't catch us up.

The four of us — Senhor Valter and his glamorous wife, Dona Judite, the little boys, Derek and Neil — fell out of time.

Several nights ago, I went out alone bottom bouncing for walleye here on Lake of the Woods, in my boat, *Tardelli*, a 2016 18.5 foot Lund Impact, battleship grey, 115 HP Honda 4-stroke, Minn Kota Ulterra trolling motor, remote-controlled. Two livewells. Lots of storage space for rods. Hummingbird depthfinder. A sultry windless evening in our pandemic summer, threatening the rain that came the next day. The water darker, the way walleye like it, with their large sensitive eyes. First I caught a large pike, well over twenty pounds. I manhandled it into the boat, took photos, one of them of the fish unable to fit within the 38-inch metal ruler I carry. Then I lowered the fish back into the water, where it righted itself and finned down, wavered out of sight.

The walleye were there in plenty. I caught five, let the smallest one go, brought them back and filleted them.

Long ago, when we fished for bluefish, puxa puxa (poosha poosha, as I have said, or pull, pull), the line wore small cuts into our index fingers, which became calloused. I was proud of this.

Now Tardelli grins at my clumsy passes with the filleting knife. Flicking the ash from his unfiltered Continental with his third, fourth finger.

Ninety-eight now, Senhor Valter watches the major tennis tournaments on TV at their strange hours in Rio and reports the scores to me long distance on the phone. Having spent his childhood in Zagreb, he's a Djokovic fan. I prefer Federer.

DONA
JUDITE

As a child, your experience of home was so laced with terror that when, later, eventually, you were freed ("were freed?" — *became free*) to think, to write at least this much — freed enough at least to see that in that childhood, so hard to escape — actually, you can't escape, and your memories of it act like curare — you realized you'd been perennially crowded out, nowhere more threatened with random dangers than at home, from parents, from your older brother. Danger when they sparred. Danger when they turned their blare of attention on you.

Consequently, your adult life, seen through your adult eyes, which have always been acquired just now, which always might and often do close — this life will always seem safer, more secure than that former life.

This perverse reversal — this experience of feeling safer out in the world, later, now, after that first constant catastrophe of childhood, carries you through every living instance. But in another lingering syntactical effect, it impels you to question, instantly, your every response, every intuition, even, especially, this one: every sentence instantly repeated, interrupted, or endlessly qualified, mid-sentence, by your own in-house, inbred grand inquisitor. Each thought, each phrase producing an instant replication. Echolalia.

And of course this backwards-locked story breeds a deeply ironic stance, as if that were only natural. So that sometimes, now, your friends can't tell when you're being straight; sometimes, neither can you.

Neither can I, that is. Your friends, my friends. Mon semblable, mon frère, mon hypocrite lecteur. Yes, okay, bowdlerized Baudelaire. Here we are, dear reader. Or, moronically, tautologically, *It's what it is.* Gangsters like Joe Pesci in *The Irishman* to Robert De Niro, asking him to tell Al Pacino, to warn James Hoffa: "It's what it is."

Or, Nathan Detroit in Damon Runyon's *Guys and Dolls*: "Sue me, sue me / Shoot bullets through me."

Or, faux Yiddish, faux because it has always been too late: "Nu?"

So sue me, go ahead, shoot them bullets through me. I'm her son, but there's no *I*. Ai, meu Deus, Nilo. My name in Portuguese, in Brazilian lovers' mouths, *Nilo.* But since around 1990, Brazilian friends, woman or man, refuse to call me *Nilo* anymore, it's Neil. Have I betrayed them? No; it is a permanent change in the weather, south and north.

In Portuguese, ai ai is an everyday lament, every third sentence, soft commiseration. Not to be confused with aí,

there, or its street slang cognate, ali. Not to be confused
with no eye onto the world.

    I thought, quietly circling my grief, of how
    She had loved God but cursed extravagantly
    his creatures.

Thus, Irving Layton, mourning his mother, Keine Lazarovitch.
Circling Dona Judite in a sorrowing arc I see that she did not
love God, but she could certainly curse his creatures.

Senhor Valter, as I have intimated, rescued me for a
time, but at too steep a price, as I discovered, one that I
could never pay.

Gainsaying their names, the two Judiths were different
women in every way. They did not exchange husbands in
late-forties, early fifties Montreal, as one might be led to
think. Nor did the men exchange wives.

In Brazil, when we were children, Dona Judite began to
toss off what became lifelong bon mots about the twinned
names. Over the years she told dinner guests that she'd
suggested to the other Judith that they exchange napkins,
hand towels embroidered with the original initials, also
cutlery. Her guests marvelled at, applauded this insouciance.

I came to read these sallies as lines performed by her theatrical self in the one-act play she put on intermittently. Staged for her bevy of admirers in Rio, in Montreal. Staged for herself, when she was on stage.

"Hold the blow," advises King Dahfu, and of course King Dahfu is right. Nor is it sufficient to hide the blow, or to pretend there never were any, or to complain of them, or to proclaim them.

In those early years in Brazil, Derek and I played a game. By the intonation and inflection — not by content, that was cheating, so the game had to be over in the first few seconds — guess to whom Dona Judite was speaking on the phone. She was a sincere and instantaneous and unconscious mimic. She delivered to the person at the other end a speaking simulacrum of that person. Our game, we discovered, worked best when she was speaking with women. But we could guess at the men, too. Cameo or camouflage? The performances were real. All the voices were Dona Judite's. She was fluid and unknowable, most apparently to herself.

Lifelong, there have been, there were tender moments that, unnervingly, dissolved the performative Dona Judite, who resolved into my mother, who loved me. In Montreal for my fifth birthday someone gave me a big and shining blue cap pistol, an imitation Colt 45. She took it from me gently. "Sorry, no guns." Said softly, which was alarming, which caused me to cry. I was given in the gun's place a View-Master, which you clicked to see exotic and picturesque landscapes appear claustrophobically before your eyes and which I threw away as quickly as was viable.

This was when I wore a Daniel Boone coonskin cap and walked very carefully over the cracks in the sidewalk on Sherbrooke Street. I knew there were lions and tigers therein. They disported themselves in my dreams. This was when, at the kitchen table on Sherbrooke, Derek and I played with another toy gun, a Dan'l Boone frontiersman's model, pleasantly heavy to the heft, knurled and varnished wooden butt. A friend of mine from around the corner, Norman Friedman, quietly conferred with Derek. Suddenly we were in the Wild West, and I was conked with the pistol butt and ran screaming from the table.

Perhaps Dona Judite was right.

Another daily ritual emerged for us in Brazil when we moved to the rented house at 126 Codajás in Leblon from the apartment in Copacabana. We were eight or nine. 1958. At day's open, it was vital to discern Dona Judite's state of mind. *Is she in a good mood?* We whispered our guesses to each other, proffered and weighed the evidence. Much depended on this assessment. Wednesday morning's might be moot by the afternoon. A remark on Tuesday morning might be contradicted that evening. Sudden squalls that arose without warning. Senhor Valter's infinitely measured, reasoned presence; Dona Judite's storms, her cold and ominous silences. Translucent white anger.

At the small rented house on 126 Codajás Dona Judite and Senhor Valter lived in a closed-off suite, bedroom, dressing room, and bathroom, closed off by a blank white door. In the morning the door was knocked upon by a sober maid in sandals with a gleaming tray of coffee and orange juice. Hard, crisp slap of sandals carrying uniformed maids back down the hall and then down the back stairs into the kitchen. Dona Judite, in full North American crispness, saws her way through lushness that watches her with a moist earth brown eye, watches her quick blocky parade down the carpeted front stairs that twist to the ground floor. She briskly bangs out the screen door. Her heels clip down the stone stairs to the gate. The car door slams, the chauffeur eases away. Pad, pad, the maids are talking, their brown feet in old white sandals have red polish on the nails. I go down to the kitchen to make a sandwich and take an apple for Tardelli, who is, as I have said, Floriana's lover.

Meanwhile, in every season, Dona Judite sits in eternal repose. The serene set of her face belies its theatric mobility. The elaborately cocked eyebrow, saying everything, so admired by her audiences. The rehearsed gesture with a mentholated Salem, the small cough, swirl of Scotch, delicate sip, clink of ice.

The men followed her moves everywhere. Senhor Valter approved because she was his wife, charming, brilliant, radiant. *Mrs. Dalloway*. But unlike Mrs. Dalloway, Dona Judite is only eternally present because she is eternally absent. There she was, but here she is.

On Sunday, the Portuguese nanny's day off, Derek and I attend to the two little children, Michael and Jo-Anne.

"Boys! Keep it down!" calls Dona Judite from her bedroom. Senhor Valter reads that week's *Time* magazine in the small front garden.

In the Winter Garden, Michael asks us: "Now that I have my palhaços," — Portuguese for clowns, what he's decided to call the jokers we've given him to play with from a deck of cards — "what should I do with them?"

"You should take your palhaços and shove them."

"Shove them?" He is three.

Her servants fear Dona Judite, but later, they titter in the kitchen. I adore them all. Floriana the cook, Tardelli's lover, endures the longest, inhabits both houses, the small rented house at 126 Codajás and the big house at 549 that Senhor Valter has built in the later sixties, around the corner and up the hill. Later still she cooks on occasion for Senhor Valter and Rochelle at their condo in Leme, until she dies in the mid-2000s. In my early twenties, she gives me a plastic ashtray with an inset photograph of the city, a lembrança do Rio, a memento of Rio, which I have preserved, scotch-taped. It has outlasted her as things outlast us, and it is a redolent thing. Smiling, she inhabits the room; now she's dressed in her tight-fitting light brown slacks to walk to market day from the little house on Codajás. The street eyes her, openly. She knows that I know about Tardelli although neither of us mentions it. She casually allows, giggling, as we watch a soap opera one evening, that another maid, there for a few months, then gone, não regula muito bem, isn't quite right in the head. She has a small, faded gold tooth that appears when she grins; she is exceedingly pretty, a lush prettiness that endures over decades. She has aged well. She is a regular in the photos I have kept. A family familiar, gone strange to me fifty years ago, but always here.

The maids, the domestics, the servants; Dona Judite cheerfully called them "the slaves." She said it for effect. Effect upon whom?

Dona Judite's drivers: Abilio Beniches, of Spanish extraction, who began with her in Copacabana and moved with the family to Leblon. He was followed for short-lived stints by lanky Sidney, an ex-motorcycle cop who was not sufficiently deferential, although he did make an earnest attempt, which doomed him; by Ronaldo, wild-eyed and not sufficiently well-groomed; and finally by Aridalto, who came to Dona Judite at the big house at 549 Codajás, and after fifteen years there, followed her to her condo in São Conrado for the last twenty, and to whom she willed her car. Who was with the family the night in 1983 that Dona Judite's son Michael died; he told me later that in the moment, "alguma coisa deu nas minhas pernas," something suddenly happened to his legs, preventing him from walking. Dona Judite's most faithful, if fearful companion. Capable of quiet wry observations, in unguarded moments, about her wrath.

There were evenings in the Winter Garden in the small house — in my early teens I amused myself by thinking, Winter Garden for Brazilian winter evenings, home from boarding school in the U.S. for June, July, August — when Derek and I played Scrabble with another, more fanciful Dona Judite. With her pencil — she was keeping score in her impeccable hand — she drew, deftly, nine whiskered cartoon cats for the nine Besner siblings by birth order, one of them my father, then labelled each with its name. Then she named their spouses, added brief histories; named their children, more stories. Named the Besner patriarch and matriarch, Mama and Papa, J.A., Joseph Alter, a.k.a. The Judge. Who, as my father in Montreal advised years later, was thus named because he dispensed advice much sought after on St. Laurent, a.k.a. the Main.

Then, shifting gears suddenly, Dona Judite tells us the clincher, how she had *marched in* to the house on Elm Avenue (*Ellum* Avenue) to tell Mama Besner that she was divorcing her son Morty. Yes, she was. Firmly, no-nonsense, that's that. Her version of *It's what it is*. We were a rapt audience. Still looking at the nine named cats, their slender whiskers.

In the Winter Garden, on another evening close by, nursing her Scotch at the same table, a barbeque in progress, she complains quietly to me about Senhor Valter. Who does not pay any attention to her. Who could leave, she says, at a moment's notice; who has four hangers arranged precisely in his closet, and one small suitcase. Who could talk to princes, she allowed, but no longer conversed with her.

Did Senhor Valter leave her, or did Dona Judite leave him? It is said that she left him twice in those early years in Brazil, moved back with her boys twice to Montreal, returned twice to Brazil. But we did not know that. We knew only that we moved, twice, to Montreal, and returned twice, some months later, to Brazil.

In our thirties, in Canada, Senhor Valter told us his version of those departures and returns. Dona Judite never said a word. But here she is in the late fifties in Montreal, December, in a place we have rented for six months on Upper Trafalgar, calling us, Derek and Neil, to an upstairs window to show us a fresh skiff of snow on the grass: "Well boys, what do you think of that?" she asks us lightly in the tone of minor-key wonderment she can summon. There is no hint of the reason we have come to Montreal, nor the reason that some months later we return to Brazil, this time the four of us on a day-long plane ride in a Constellation that alights in Spanish-speaking airports before arriving into Portuguese once again. But harrying the edges of the Montreal skiff of snow, before the long flight through sunlight, I hear her quietly crying one night down the hall on Trafalgar, "Walter, I don't want to go back," met with indistinct male murmuring, soothing.

We do know that from the Winter Garden in the small house on Codajás, on another evening a few years later, we hear her suddenly erupt in terrible screaming at Senhor Valter, before we hear the French Canadian nanny from Quebec, Beatrice LePage, trying to calm her, and we watch

Senhor Valter descend the stairs and enter the Winter Garden to play with Michael, to calm him, Dona Judite sobbing terribly upstairs. Derek and I tell him, later, our thought: *If she was that furious with him, what would she possibly be like with us?* Momentarily, we grin, a conspiracy of three.

Here is Dona Judite in the Brazilian winter, late June 1965, a few weeks before I board the *Ponta Negra* for my forty-five-day educational furlough, sitting at the yacht club in the soft sun of a late afternoon with her American friend Pat Barnett. These ghosts: soon after, Pat Barnett vanished back to Oklahoma to raise horses, for reasons connected to her husband's leaving her in Rio for another woman.

The women wear large dark sunglasses against the glare. I am returning with Tardelli from fishing. The women have small cafezinhos in front of them, strong Brazilian coffee. It is now called espresso, in one of the legion Brazilian feints, which I lament in my toxic nostalgia, at becoming more European, at becoming more American. In reality the coffee has not changed.

I am, this once, to get a lift home with Dona Judite. Tardelli and I will not slide down as usual to the far gritty concrete docks near the warehoused boats and the sailors' lockers. I manoeuver to the main landing under the green and yellow Brazilian flag, Ordem e Progresso, Order and Progress, and step off the boat. Used condoms, limp and distended, float on the surface of the water amidst streaks of oil. Tardelli pulls away.

"Who was driving the boat when you came in?" asks Dona Judite.

I tell her I was. "It slid in so gracefully." Pat Barnett agrees, smiles. We leave the club in Dona Judite's American car, still rare in those days. Her driver is now Abilio Beniches. He is possessed of a horse cock. Derek and I saw him, mornings, when he slept in our bedroom, our caretaker for two weeks as Dona Judite and Senhor Valter went to Europe for reasons unknown. Years later we learned that Abilio was having it off with the children's Portuguese nursemaid, Carmina, successor to Beatrice LePage. Years later still, long after his employ with Dona Judite, we learned that he keeled over at breakfast, a brain hemorrhage, in a botequim, a corner bar in Leblon. Had any of us been able to mark this sad occasion as it deserved, perhaps we could have begun to re-enter time.

Instead, the boat continues, perennially, to return to the yacht club in the lowering sun of a late weekday winter afternoon, and Dona Judite tells me that the boat arrived so gracefully it seemed to float above the water. Tardelli pulls away, and Abilio drives us home, drops off Pat Barnett en route at her apartment building on the border between Ipanema and Leblon. Dona Judite lights a Salem and the aroma of menthol swells in the car's interior, cooler and more sterile than the air conditioning.

She said she hated Brazil. She said she hated Portuguese,

considered it a bastard language. She never bothered to get verbs right, syntax aligned, pronunciation proximately passable, she who was so easy and fluent in French, both in Quebec and in France. But in Brazil, learning Portuguese well would have been to yield.

In all of her many cheery letters to me in my thirties and forties — for she was as constant, as resolute a letter writer as she was inconstant in person, her hand exacting, each small letter neatly, regularly, decisively, formed in bright blue ink — she referred to Brazil as "never-never land." The tone was cheerful, knowing. This was earned resignation.

For years on end, Dona Judite wrote a letter every day to a friend in Montreal, until her friend fell ill with cancer. One evening at the big house on Codajás, fortified with Scotch, Dona Judite declared to me that she would not let her friend die. We both knew this sharp defiance to be empty and we both knew she meant it. My sister and I prevented her going home that night to her condo in São Conrado, enforced her sleeping at the house from which she'd moved ten years earlier. The next morning Senhor Valter, long departed by then from those precincts, advised me on the phone that he had heard my sister and I had our hands full. Thus did Senhor Valter and Dona Judite, long separated by then, continue to monitor each other through my sister. Thus do I pull up febrile strands of time from southern space. *Up*: I forever imagine Brazil below, both powerful and quiescent. A bright shout and a liquid silence.

Dona Judite in her early years in Brazil began to write a novel. She sent the first part of the manuscript to Random House. She had a connection there. She advised me, severely, "It's not what you know, it's who you know." Upon her death, I discovered the contract from Random House and a hundred or so pages of typed manuscript on yellowing paper, along with friendly correspondence from the editor, advising her that unfortunately, when he'd presented the manuscript to his board, they, like him, had felt there needed to be major changes. Apparently Dona Judite had ignored the recommendations and abandoned the project. It was disheartening to read the yellowing pages and to see that the editor had been right. The writing was at once flip and inert, and after twenty pages I had to put it down. She never mentioned the novel.

In Montreal, she'd written advertising jingles for the radio; she'd worked as a model. In Brazil, she taught modelling at the little house on Codajás to a group of young American girls, teenagers — taught them how to stand, pose, turn — issuing a throaty offhand goodbye to her teenaged son hurrying out of the house to catch the bus and go fishing with Tardelli. Catching, out of the corner of one eye, the girls. Who were enchanted with Dona Judite.

Her father told me in Montreal, gravely, when I was in my later teens, "Your mother is very talented." That is how her friends and relatives in Montreal remember her. "An inspiration." Exerting a sparking allure: as Senhor Valter put it, "Half of Montreal was after her."

She hated Brazilian primitive art. She was contemptuous, and vocally so, of Brazilian politics, of the economy, the runaway inflation. Of the people. In the small house at 126 Rua Codajás that we rented beginning in 1958 in Leblon, which was then a far and quiet suburb, but which is now more upscale than Ipanema, more chic than Copacabana, which has become rundown and dirty, she papered the inside of the downstairs bathroom door, just off the kitchen, with lacquered one cruzeiro bills.

This embarrassed me for her, but it did not embarrass her.

She threw a costume party at the little house. She dressed as a one-way ticket to Montreal. Hilarity from her admiring guests, the expatriate and diplomatic community. She hired a talented singer and guitarist to play bossa nova and samba, standing in doorways, strolling through the living room. It was thought emancipated that he was Black. Dona Judite asked him if he would give me lessons. He would be honoured. He drank her Scotch, he vomited profusely in the garden, and slipped away.

From the corner store two blocks away on Venâncio Flores, I bought her chocolate caramels made by Behring, wrapped individually in crinkled blue wax paper with tidy white dots. These cost one crumpled green-blue cruzeiro note each. The same notes as those lacquered on the back of the bathroom door.

The proprietor from Portugal lifted out a handful of the candies from a glass bowl on the countertop, counted them. I brought them to her after fishing, into her glacial bedroom, where she would raise an eyebrow, ask me what these were for. For nothing, I mumbled. I was thirteen.

White was her colour then. Whitewashed walls, white furniture, everything sterile white. Like the smoke from her Salems. Even the crystal seemed to gleam and sparkle white, the ice cubes in her evening Scotch, transparent white, clear and clicking.

She towered over my brother and me in the late fifties and early sixties, but now I believe that even then she sensed, as she began to sink slowly through her cold white anger, softened only by her ever more deeply hued sorrow, that she was often, in her many-chambered heart, "um carneiro," a lamb, as Erik Kreuger put it — Senhor Valter's Swedish associate, who rented the little house in the later sixties.

When I was fifteen, she was forty. Senhor Valter, forty-three. The mind stumbling, wet amidst time's tears. García Márquez: "Life is not what one lived, but what one remembers and how one remembers it in order to recount it."

I remember everything, obsessively. Borges has a story in *Labyrinths* about a man who could not cease from remembering, "Funes the Memorious."

But that is a fable. Funes ain't got nothin' on me. *It's what it is.* If Dona Judite at the Chinese restaurant that night in Leblon was right, if mystery has gone out of the world, and if that happened so long, long ago, then memory becomes impossibly burdened, the past unfairly freighted, and the present unimaginable. Atwood wanted only *this.*

She wants *this*. But in order to arrive at *this*, you must not succumb to amnesia, and we are all amnesiacs.

The cure for amnesia is not memory, and memory is not a parlour game. It has nothing to do with facts or with what *really* happened.

Memory is a fugue. But if you don't, if you can't or you won't remember, what's to be done with your life?

In 1983 Dona Judite suffered the loss of her son Michael, and, beginning far earlier, she suffered her carefully and precisely managed abandonment by Senhor Valter, staged over the course of twenty years. It could not have been seen by either of them in this way, for it is also true that they loved each other. They were each other's "Pussycat." They had embarked together for Brazil. They had left Montreal ("that provincial backwater"). They had two new children, whom, fatally, they loved. They also, nearly fatally, loved us, Derek and Neil.

What does intention have to do with it? For they did have loving intentions, although with lethal effects.

When I called her in Rio from Canada on learning of Michael's death, I became tongue-tied. I asked, "How do you feel?"

"Oh, how can I feel?" Anguished, from five thousand miles.

Here is Dona Judite in the little garden in São Conrado, April 2003, three months before her own death. She moved to this building soon after Michael's death in 1983, when Senhor Valter became immobilized in his captain's chair outside by the pool at the big house at 549 Codajás. That August of 1983, Michael had been classified Number 1 in his category of motorcycles in Rio, racing the 125cc machines that he helped to build. He died after a car crash late one night. He was returning from midnight mass to celebrate an anniversary of Netumar, Senhor Valter's shipping company. Swerving to avoid a streetcleaner, he hit a lamppost. He died early that morning on the operating table.

In the early seventies, having been schooled by a Rabbi in Rio, Michael was brought to Montreal for his Bar Mitzvah: the power of Dona Judite's parents. He is a chubby boy; Derek and I are at the airport a few days later, seeing the four of them off as they return to Rio, Dona Judite, Senhor Valter, and their two children, Michael Lorne Gainsbury and Jo-Anne Rochelle Gainsbury. Away from the others, Michael falls into a moment of tears with his older half-brothers, who believe that they understand his distress at returning to prison.

Thus do we revisit our lives, our feelings, upon others. We do not really understand. We see him crying, and the rest is inference, but based upon which data? Upon what we feel, each of us? As if, to begin with, that were the same?

Our attempts to comfort him are clumsy.

"So you abandoned your little brother and your little sister in Rio," suggests a psychologist at the University of Waterloo that Derek, now himself a psychologist, has suddenly seduced me into seeing with him, as if by chance, as we tour his campus. We're in our late thirties; these sudden ambushes have long been a favourite tactic, inspired by his own urgent needs. *Abandoned them?* We who understood ourselves when we were young men as having fled Brazil, as having fled the family, north and south, entirely.

Abandoned or not, Michael in his late teens, early twenties, understands Dona Judite well enough to say to his older half-brothers in Brazil on one of our visits, Essa foi boa, that was a good one, at one of Dona Judite's sallies. Looking sidelong at us, grinning, shaking his head. *That much he knows*, we think. But this does not save him or Dona Judite from themselves.

Now it's April 2003, twenty years since he died, and Dona Judite and I sip diet cokes in the little ground-floor garden in the condominium building in São Conrado where she has lived since shortly after Michael's death, leaving her grown daughter in the big house. A large blue butterfly flaps its large wings slowly, magisterially, passes us at eye level, and I am immediately transposed to our little garden in the back yard of the little rented house at 126 Rua Codajás, where I saw my first morpho. Slow magic, at once fluid and instantaneous. The first morpho is the same one, there's always only one, they are always too big, outsized. Like the Brazilian blades of grass, too thick.

"There is no wing like meaning," advises Wallace Stevens, but of course he means something else. The butterflies' passings, one over the other, convey nothing like meaning. I remain trapped in the literal along that southern littoral. I'm ten or eleven and I am forty-three, sitting with Dona Judite in her condo's ground-floor garden. Time has recessed within the self-same place. Or is it the reverse?

There were, as I have said, two moves for the new family in Brazil, one from the Copacabana apartment to the smaller rented house at 126 Codajás in Leblon in 1957, and one from the rented house to the big house Senhor Valter has built to Dona Judite's specifications, to which the family moved in 1966. But by then Derek and I have embarked on our own escapes, via university in Florida, in LA. We have begun to encircle with wariness our annual, twice-annual returns to Brazil. Each arrival, each departure more fraught. On the day of one departure in my thirties I cannot sit still, I circle the house endlessly, inside, outside; I watch the little brown lizards on the whitewashed walls over the pool, immobile until they move in the blink of an eye. Pick one up, and it drops its tail and escapes.

I tried to write poems about this terrible restlessness, about the lizards. Thank god I have destroyed them.

Although in April 2003 I remark on the butterfly to my mother, giving her its scientific name — *Morpho* — I stop short of remembering for her its predecessor's passing, forty years earlier. Instead I tell her that I remember our little house at 126 Codajás, the back yard, how I loved it, how important it was. I am near tears, but she doesn't notice. That's not her fault. Dona Judite is dying of kidney disease, she has other things on her mind. "Of course, those were your formative years," she says to me. Sternly.

The moment passes, but it never passes. We fail to connect. I will circle her forever.

In her last years, therefore, when I am in Brazil and visit her most late afternoons for a Scotch in her condo, I have grown impatient with her, I interrupt her stories, I badger her, speak over her, cut her short. I interrogate her about the past, about Montreal; her memory for fifty, sixty years earlier is better than for yesterday, for last year.

I reprimand myself but I cannot stop this peremptory, almost dismissive behaviour, and Dona Judite, a small person now, has begun to lose her name. Long distance as in person, I begin to address her as "Mother" in a commanding and sententious tone. I have become grave with her, almost hectoring. She who terrified us and inspired such scurrying fear in her maids in the late fifties, she who commandeered instant attention, who inspired their murmuring obedience: "Sim, Dona Judite," or a more hurried "Sim, senhora" when more abasement was required. Now I hector her despite myself. I don't let her complete her answers, but she doesn't notice.

She lights another Salem. Her doctor at the dialysis clinic has advised her to stop smoking, given her careful instructions as to diet, as to some limited exercise. I go to the clinic with her six months before her death to meet with the doctor, who repeats, slowly, carefully, all the instructions she has given my mother. The doctor is solicitous, generous. But when I repeat the instructions to my mother later that day, slowly and carefully, and then ask her if she'll follow them, she reverts, quickly, to an earlier Dona Judite. "No." Quickly, airily, brightly tossed off. She is gamin; she is La Belle Dame Sans Merci du Quebec en Brésil, a coquette playing to her bevy of admirers — but wait, it's only her adult son now. Still, "No." She is, after all, Judith Gainsbury. She remains, sparkling, at the centre of the room. Is this *genuine*, is this *really her*? Well, yes, it is she.

She was a victim of her own charm.

When I am lost in Montreal at twenty-one, she and I go out to dinner on one of her flying visits up from "never-never land." I confide to her that I think maybe I'll go to Africa. "Well, go. Just go," she tells me. I drink this in. It is uttered with frankness, with sincerity, quietly but casually, in the throaty plangent voice she draws upon for these occasions. She means it; she means well. I recognize, from Brazilian dinners a few years earlier, her and me, that she is about to confide something further, something important, and she does: "You know, Neil, you remind me of Lazzie. You're just like him." Her older brother Lazarus, who threw himself out a New York hotel room before I was born, heartbroken about being dumped by his show-business lady there. "He was psychotic," she informs me, offhand, on other occasions. "When Lazzie died, my father didn't know what to do with himself. He held out his hand for my mother to cut his nails," she told me.

When she tells me I remind her of Lazzie, she intends no harm. This is her version of herself as casual but deep truth-teller. In April 2003, I find a faded clipping from her suitcase, advising that the Montreal nightclub scene is mourning the sudden passing of "Laz" Cohen, who was known to hop behind the bar on a busy night to help out. I have preserved the clipping. At her younger brother David's shivah in Montreal in 2010, I learn more about Lazzie from David's friends. The woman from New York was forbidden entrance, was required by David's parents, Lazzie's and Judith's, to stand across the street from the house on Westmount Avenue, in the little park there. My grandfather, I am told, approached a friend of David's then, asked him to come and live with them at the house for a few months. He was worried about his surviving son. David's friend acquiesced.

These stories, from that Montreal, from that house on the southeast corner of Argyle and Westmount Avenue, lap gently at its battlements, which become shaded over once again, and then again, with this soft ivy of loss. As if this might become a House of Usher, as if it might fall, not into Poe's dark tarn, but sliding, rather, down that colder steep slope from near the top of Westmount, carrying its residents, along with thousands of others on these southern heights of Mount Royal, in a slow swoon down the snowcooled hills onto Sherbrooke Street, or east into Côte Saint-Luc, taking a new direction, reversing their ascent not so long ago from Saint Urbain and environs. For these generations have slid down the mountainside. They have fallen, slower than the snow.

As I have said, Derek and I dubbed this redoubt near the top of Argyle "the Ponderosa," my mother's father and mother "Happy Horace" and "Joyous Jennie," my mother's surviving brother "Dubious David."

But we, too, fell away from it, we fell away from them.

Rather, they fell away from us: in my thirties I began to see them in a greying daylight, at once leaning backwards and reaching towards me with outstretched arms in mute supplication, their mouths slightly open in a gentle *O*; they visited me for years on end in this guise, in another, more intimate version of that generalized falling away, that swooning down those hills.

I can, readily, summon my grandparents' images now, but they do not arise of their own decorous accord, in that stately rhythm, as they did before. There is no madeleine, and they do not arrive voluntarily, although occasionally I still overhear a phrase passing between them; there arises a faint sweet but indeterminate scent, a rustling of my grandmother's clothes. Here she is standing in her back yard, in her later eighties: "It goes so fast, Neil."

For her part, Dona Judite remains immediate, in the foreground, on the march, refusing the gentle blurring that attends the others' repose.

On her fly-in visits to the Ponderosa over the years my mother steps briskly away from her name in Portuguese. She exclaims over "the pace" here in the North. When I am twenty, lost and mad, having returned to Montreal from LA, she proffers advice before she leaves to return to

Brazil: "Neil, do yourself a favour. Stop thinking." She and Derek urge me to consult a psychiatrist. But I wish to speak with her then about Henry Miller's book of essays, *The Wisdom of the Heart*. I want to praise his high enthusiasm for Goethe — "Everything nourished him," Miller writes. He writes in another essay that the long way is, ultimately, the shortest way; I wish to exalt this advice, to expound upon this truth, but Dona Judite is already on her way back to never-never land.

Dona Judite's first cousin is Leonard Cohen, who tells me in those years that "your mother has been an inspiration to me." But Dona Judite in Brazil dismisses him: "Oh Neil, he's such a poser."

Years later a cultural anthropologist in Winnipeg explains to me that Cohen is in fact my first cousin once removed and that I should not worry over it. By then, I've been reading him, singing his songs for years. When he attends my grand-parents' fiftieth wedding anniversary party in Montreal in the early seventies, thrown by Dona Judite's brother David at his large Westmount home, I tell him I like his work very much, that *he* has inspired me. I don't mention my mother's dismissal of him in Brazil. I spend an afternoon with him at his house on Saint Dominique; he is fasting that day, eating pills.

He is warm to me, wryly resigned about the family: "Aren't they wonderful?"

Quietly, selectively, I try to trade on our relation. In Winnipeg I write a song, successful, for a lover:

I told you that you looked like
A Suzanne just in from Norway
And your eyes were green with all the seas
    you sailed on
Then I sang you all those Cohen songs
And held you in the evening
But in the morning there was some test
    that we both failed on.

I began to miss you before we met
It's part of learning to regret
What you can't have before it's slipping
    through your fingers
Yes I know you have to go, your future
    lovers keep on whispering
How they'll kiss you long and slow, the
    memory lingers

I wrote him an apologia pro imitatio horribilis, never sent:

I'm sorry that I've come here with this
    heavy gong of gloom
I'm sorry that I've brought this heavy
    weight into the room
I'm sorry for the angels that must listen to
    this song
I'm sorry that I've gotten everything so
    very wrong

To myself I quote for years his description of my grandfather, Happy Horace, from *The Favorite Game:* "A Victorian gentleman of Hebraic persuasion." I quote to myself his description of his graduate studies at Columbia, "Our hands, bloody with commas."

Reading, writing: three years later, in the big house on Codajás where by this time I have become, for good, a guest, Dona Judite sets up a card table in the guest bedroom so that I can type up my master's thesis on Saul Bellow. I have with me two green and yellow paperbacks, volumes 1 and 2 of D.H. Lawrence's collected stories. Reading them — "The Horse Dealer's Daughter," "The Rocking Horse Winner" — I fall into a glowering silence that alarms Dona Judite. "What's wrong?" she asks me on the stairs, but I am unable to provide an explanation. I am unable to separate literature and life.

Her tastefully appointed library downstairs in the big house held the leatherbound Franklin collection of world masterpieces. It was here, as I mentioned earlier, that I fell into Kafka's *Letter to His Father*, which shot a spike of adrenaline up my back. On one visit in the seventies I found myself imprisoned for nights on end within the guest bedroom, the room that looked down on the swimming pool, by Solzhenitsyn's *In the First Circle*. That was the era of hours-long midnight walks to Copacabana and back, murmuring, going out and returning, boa noite to the armed guard who now presided at the gate. Kidnappings were in vogue.

But in that same guest bedroom twenty-five years later I awoke at early sunrise one morning to see Corcovado *alive*, sending its radiant dark green and dark brown breath pulsing down its singing and sunlit flank. It was *alive*. Spinoza was right.

Whom could I tell? I told the psychologist back in Winnipeg, he who had asked me about vision quests. I talked to him about exaltation. We sat across from each other, grinning.

These transports in Brazil: one afternoon, I boarded a bus from Leblon to Copacabana. I was twelve. The bus lurched in the sun amidst loud traffic, the scent of gas and diesel. Looking around at the passengers I saw that *we are all alive*. I looked around again. No change, except within: *We are alive! We are, all of us, alive. Here we are.*

Presence: Atwood wants only *this*. It is communal, and it is always. Time falling away. God is alive, magic is afoot.

Or, walking on Siqueira Campos in the sunlight, a busy Copacabana thoroughfare leading down from the beach towards Botafogo. The sidewalk is busy. I'm fifteen. Furling her blue skirt, a joyful woman, her face lit, beaming, sails past me. She is abundant, bursting with manifest energy, full breasts bountiful beneath her blue top. No name can ever stop her. Sailing on the sidewalk.

I could not have told Dona Judite about Corcovado, or

that we are all alive, or, a few years later, about the woman in blue. To our mutual detriment, we lacked the vocabulary and the wavelength. But I could tell her, one evening in the library, of my inordinate fondness for *The Swiss Family Robinson*, and she could allow that she could readily see why that story of a marooned family cheerfully, resourcefully making do, could so captivate me. But why, then, was I moved, that same evening, to quietly announce to her that I knew that she believed that freethinking was a dodge? Thus did we, do we circle each other. "Yes, I do," she said.

As I continue, brusquely, to interrogate Dona Judite in Brazil in her last years, she continues to impart new information to me. I show her another faded *Montreal Gazette* clipping that she has preserved from the forties, layered among the letters I had discovered in the suitcase and which I was forbidden to read or to take. I stole it as well. She confirms the clipping's terse report that my uncle Aaron Besner, my father's older brother, was indicted in the forties for racketeering in Detroit. I check with Senhor Valter. He cheerfully confirms this detail. Another dimming scrim rises up, north; but my father in Montreal has been gone for almost a decade, and I cannot see very far up into that gentle smoky distance. Nor do I wish to ask my first cousin in Montreal, Aaron's son, about this. Let sleeping racketeers lie. With a fedora turned up at the brow, with a cigar, with the rubbers the men in Montreal wore over their shoes in the slush in that era, in that sepia memory.

My rudeness notwithstanding, these conversations with Dona Judite are more felt, for both of us, than any I have ever had with Senhor Valter. Despite ourselves, we often succeed, Senhor Valter and I, at laughing together, at floating, embalmed, in the cheap, falsely sweet perfume of shared nostalgia. That is the best we can do. For her part Dona Judite surprises over the years with sudden warmth, with a sharp intuition, inhabiting for an instant, then another, an incarnation, an intimation of another person standing alongside her, aslant.

Attending the blue butterfly's elegant progress in her condo's little garden as we sip our diet cokes, a silent precinct ever arises. Over the low whitewashed wall in the back yard of our little rented house at 126 Codajás in the late 1950s in Leblon stands a vacant lot, and in the lot stands a low brown tree, a goiabeira, a guava tree. I have been taught by the moleques, the street kids, that the forks of the goiabeira make the best slingshots, and they do. The wood is a rich and supple brown. I make a slingshot with a forquilha, a fork cut from the goiabeira, and arm the forquilha with strips of thick red rubber cut from the inner tube of a truck tire, scrounged from a bicycle repair shop off Ataulfo de Paiva. The thick red rubber from the inner tubes of truck tires is the best. Strips cut from bicycle inner tubes, with their thin black rubber, do not stretch with a sufficiently elastic snap. The red strips from the truck tires' inner tube can be tied to the forquilha with thin white string, or with much thinner strips of rubber, but not with fishing line because it cuts into the rubber.

The pouch for the slingshot is made from an old piece of shoe leather and the rocks are picked up off the street. É pecado matar andorinha, it's a sin to kill a swallow, but I am full of stealthy wordless rage arrived from nowhere, and I kill birds of many species, swallows, once a hummingbird sitting in a moment of stillness on a telephone wire, the pardal, a sparrow, rolinhas, the little brown doves, yellow bem-te-vis, tyrant flycatchers. Google it: *The Great Kiskadee*. I kill cicadas early in the morning. It takes a good shot to hit one where it lies flat against a tree trunk. Later, in the heat, they trill, the thin shrill music welling up and overlapping in waves. As if they were kin to the Portuguese knife sharpeners who patrol the streets, grinding whining metal against the whetstone.

On my last morning home from summer camp in the mountains outside Rio, in Teresópolis — I have been brought down to spend a few days with my grandmother, visiting from Montreal, she of those mysterious utterances in her kitchen, "That irresponsible pair, the two of them" — I go out early, seized with a surge in my wordless rage, and kill five birds before Abilio drives us back to the mountains.

Derek and I mount a guerrilla slingshot war in the thick forest at the back of our American friends' house around the corner on Codajás, two militias of two, each guerilla unit pairing a brother from each family, stalking each other. Derek appears suddenly five feet in front of me, aims and fires. The rock catches me just under the eye, but he hasn't stretched the rubber back far enough, he is awkward with this new weapon. He knows, however, that I know his intent. We glare. Our friends' father breaks up the war, there is a sullen armistice.

This among other signs is why, I infer years later, Dona Judite one afternoon takes Derek to a psychologist. This is strange in Brazil in 1959. This is why, I infer, although nothing is said, Derek is taken from The British School of Rio and resituated in Our Lady of Mercy for his final two years.

We have fist fights into our twenties.

Dona Judite is at times unnervingly prescient: she remarks to me quietly one evening over her Scotch in the little house that "if he stands the gaffe Derek will become a brilliant psychologist." I don't know what "gaffe" means. "You will be a teacher," she continues.

Over the years I heard, north and south, "Your mother is brilliant," but that does not capture it; nor did her doctor in Brazil, early 2000s, when it was first discovered her kidneys were failing. Shaking his head he said to me, admiringly, "Com aquela mente ela não se conforma," with that mind of hers she won't go along with anything. Likewise Senhor Valter confines himself to a small shake of his head at her evident brilliance. Which does not prevent him from lamenting, as the three of us drive down Copacabana beach one evening during Carnaval and he points to the happy crowds, the bright clothes, the samba — I am in my early teens — "Judie, why must you always ruin everything," when she comments, "That's what you get from an ignorant populace." From the back seat, I inhale tone, timbre, and the pregnant silence that follows.

Admiring the craft of my homemade slingshots and marvelling at my skill, Senhor Valter calls me David, "Like David and Goliath," he tells me. The street kids, the moleques, are better shots than me and they carry the birds in pouches, to eat later. "Tá rindo ou tá chorando," are you laughing or crying, a bunch asks me when their football almost catches me midriff as I come home off the bus one schoolday afternoon. I'm eleven. I defend myself with my schoolbag.

I do not doubt that by their lights, Dona Judite loved me, that Senhor Valter loved me. But there was too much interference. Too much travel, drowning time in oceans impossible to fathom.

Everyone was crowded out. We all began to unknow each other too early. John Irving's phrase, from *The World According to Garp*.

They both warned me in those years, in these years, shaking their heads, intoning in mock but real despair a sorrowing and anti-lyrical refrain that flows across time:

"Get your head out of the clouds." One of the very few phrases of Dona Judite's that Senhor Valter adopted. Or, "You don't have the brains God gave a goose." Or, "You would lose your head if it wasn't nailed on."

Dona Judite liked to tell stories to friends in Rio about me as a little child in Montreal. "One day he walked straight into a lamppost, bloodied his face. Did you ever?" Or, "He went missing. I found him an hour later, sitting with a big smile in the flower patch across Sherbrooke in front of City Hall." The tag "Did you ever?" was delivered marvelling. Incredulous. Look at that child; also, look at me.

But they both learned new phrases as well. In the early eighties they surprised me when both learned to use "hassle" without appearing awkward. In 2003, a few months before her death, Dona Judite said to me in her condo, speaking of the people sitting with her in the waiting room on her twice-weekly visits to the dialysis clinic in Botafogo, that this was "a reality check" for her. Glancing at me to see if I'd heard her deploy the phrase.

In her loving mother's guise, which was also real, Dona Judite took me as a young teenager to shows in Montreal — The Kingston Trio, Mort Sahl, Shelley Berman. She took me to see *Beyond the Fringe* in New York. She, who was not overly fond of travel by sea, took me on an overnight trip down the coast to São Paulo; she hated snakes but took me when I was twelve to world famous Butantan there, waiting in the taxi while I toured the place. Derek and I, engrossed, played her Lenny Bruce albums over and again in the Winter Garden. On one occasion she took me downtown in Rio, bought me a Trini Lopez album. "Lemon tree, very pretty." In the fall of 1962, she spent six hours at Macy's with me in New York, outfitting me for boarding school.

That November 1962, dressed for this occasion in Montreal in a custom-fitted morning suit by my grandfather, proprietor of a clothing business, I was Bar Mitzvah. He had ordered me to stop playing guitar and singing the evening before, I would ruin my voice. The following Monday morning Dona Judite took us, Derek and Neil, to New York on Eastern Airlines, thence by limo to the Jewish boarding school in Stamford, Connecticut, that we attended for the ensuing four years. When I came down the stairs from the dormitory to say goodbye to her, she was gone.

At the time I was nonplussed. Over the years I came to accuse her in my heart of heartlessness until other images arose, insistent, in which it was *she* who could not bear to say goodbye.

Another image unspools itself alongside: when she takes Derek, her firstborn, to the airport in Rio to see him off to Montreal for his Bar Mitzvah, for his months of preparation at the synagogue, living with his grandparents, I am standing beside her on a rainy morning at Galeão, the old airport now long out of commission. You could stand outside on the balcony then, overlooking the tarmac. Jets were new in the world: Pan American was still the standard. Umbrella raised over us, she stood very still for long moments, watched the plane taxi and take off. Then she turned to me, resolute, determined — *about what?* — and marched us back out to the car. Cut to black.

Dona Judite has been gone since Thursday, July 24, 2003. My mania for days, dates: this is eight days after Carol Shields's death in Victoria, Wednesday, July 16. Dona Judite's life was arrested for its last twenty years, after Michael died in August 1983. As she wished, she was buried next to him in the hideous bald and heat-drenched Jewish cemetery in Caju in the north of Rio. On her grave, to Senhor Valter's displeasure, my sister and I have caused to be engraved "The best was barely good enough," one of her favourite tossed-off phrases, the past tense the only concession to her mortality.

At the graveside, in July winter heat, her brother David, come down from Montreal, recites Kaddish, his voice trembling over the syllables turned occult under a pagan sun. Lowering the coffin, I stumble; "com calma, senhor" murmurs one of the Brazilian gravediggers, "calmly, sir."

As ever, atemporally, a small and sullen calamity stretches over these last years. In the car a year earlier, Senhor Valter, Dona Judite's decline already foretold, asks me what would be done with the *corpse*: his usually unerring English has failed him under duress. This exchange simmers, leading to a quiet confrontation with him in a restaurant the day before I return to Canada after the funeral in Rio.

"You know, Neil, I don't like your attitude very much," he remarks quietly as a silence falls over us. "That's all right, Walter, you don't need to like my attitude," I allow in my turn, and we grin tightly at each other. Facing off at forty-five and eighty-one, this is as close as we come to our own species of genteel divorce. Over my protests, insisting as always on his exacting sense of protocol — we did not speak to each other for over a year in the midseventies over his tight-lipped fury at my lack of observance of proper airport behaviour in Vancouver following my first wedding — Senhor Valter drives me to the airport in Rio, despite our contretemps. En route, Dona Judite's *corpse* lies in ethereal state on the front seat between us as we exchange pleasantly murderous nonsense. When I am back in Winnipeg, and email Senhor Valter to advise that perhaps we will see each other when I next return to Brazil, perhaps not, he circulates the email to my siblings as testimony to my incivility.

Thus does Dona Judite preside.

When I last visited the cemetery in 2018, I was forbidden to leave flowers by the new proprietors, who sternly informed me that this was not a festive place. Dona Judite had brought flowers for twenty years to Michael's grave, and I, intermittently, to hers.

Now, however, there is a new order in Ordem e Progresso. Now, President Bolsonaro brings his own atemporal antireality to dismiss the pandemic by fiat: it's nothing, a gripezinha, a little flu. He is Donald Trump's first cousin in southern climes. Between the two countries, the deaths exceed 700,000.

Bolsonaro unwittingly destroys time, but I remain forever bent on redeeming time.

In that old order, Brazilian winter, 1965, here are Senhor Valter and Dona Judite at lunch with me in the yacht club a week before I board the *Ponta Negra*. They are worrying over me, but I am largely unconscious of their worry. They agree that if they put me aboard a Greek freighter, I will "come off buggered." It is therefore determined that Senhor Valter will put me on one of his Liberty ships, the *Caiçara*, bound for Buenos Aires, but the ship is delayed. Tight-lipped, they grip their Marlboros, their Salems; lighters snap open, snap closed. Time, as they say, is of the essence, and so I board the *Ponta Negra* in mid-July 1965.

Some time during the later years in the little house, Dona Judite resolves to learn how to cook, 1963, perhaps; I'm thirteen. Until then we have only a few fugitive memories of her cooking in the Montreal apartment on Sherbrooke Street, serving us Campbell's tomato soup and Ritz crackers. When she makes us toast rather than Rice Krispies for breakfast, I secret the crusts in a toy yellow dump truck and unload the cargo nearby, under the radiator. Pleasantly heavy, a substantial dump truck, laden furtively with contraband.

But now she has decided to cook more seriously. She commandeers the kitchen, the maids step back. She makes a beef roast, with gravy, roast potatoes. This is miraculous, Senhor Valter is impressed and we follow suit. But then, catastrophe: I hand her the silver gravy boat the wrong way and she screams, her hand badly burned. My clumsiness, my ineptness, my obliviousness have now resulted in searing injury. Senhor Valter is dispatched instantly to the pharmacy for bandages and unguent and I accompany him as he shakes his head at me, sorrowful, lips pursed, "How could you, Neil? Your mother has a serious burn." The burn heals quickly, but thus ends Dona Judite's cooking the evening meal. In later years she makes an occasional icebox cake, impossibly rich; rarely, but well, she makes wienerschnitzel, but because this was learned from a friend in Montreal, Ditte, a cheery Austrian woman who lived on our floor in that Sherbrooke apartment building — a woman whom Dona Judite called schatze, dear, but who, Dona Judite allowed in latter years, had simply vanished from her life — the wienerschnitzel did as well.

One of Dona Judite's closest woman friends from Montreal, Neri Bloomfield, visits her in Rio in the seventies, but after returning to Montreal writes to her sternly, reprimanding her for not leading a more Jewish life in Brazil. This results in the instantaneous severing of a fifty-plus-year intimate friendship. "Did you ever?" she asks me. "The nerve, the gall."

When I retired from the University of Winnipeg in 2017, I established a scholarship in Creative Writing in Dona Judite's name, the Judith Francis Gainsbury Award, to the most deserving female student. Consternation arose; designating the award for a female student only was clearly discriminatory. I held my tongue. They worked it out.

The first winner of the award in 2019 was a woman with a Portuguese surname, although her roots were in Portugal and not Brazil. She was also that year's valedictorian.

This gesture, this award in her name, would have been anathema to my mother. But this time, Dona Judite cannot get a word in.

MORT
THE
SPORT

When I begin to remember, he isn't there, although I can't remember him having left. He lives forever in Montreal, and Montreal in him.

The fervent wish first arose when I was a young teenager in Brazil and persisted for many years: *If only we had stayed in Montreal, everything would have been all right.* We first four: Dona Judite before taking on that name, Derek, and me; and, in shadow, my father. Before he became *Par*, before all his other names.

Names, these defences against relation, fending off connection. Or, inane, repeating themselves.

If only we had stayed in Montreal, then what?

Ineluctably, the wish faded. Before it became saccharine, it felt pungent, singular, strong. Before *The Swiss Family Robinson* arose to counteract it, cheery and resilient; before *The Swiss Family Robinson* arose to confirm it, too. The resourceful and loving family was *there*, was *here*, always present.

There's one answer for you, Marcel: the imagination is born in reading, and reading redeems time.

But not only in the cheery *Swiss Family Robinson*; the imagination nourishes itself reading and writing about loss. Bishop:

> the art of losing's not too hard to master
> though it may look like (*Write* it!) like
> disaster.

I thought that reading, writing about loss might soothe, might avert disaster. Name it, and thereby escape it. Nope.

Reading in English, in Brazil: the words weighed more, became more tactile if foreign, became as loud in the mind as they were silent in the world. While I was learning Portuguese in the street. Where I strolled in Leblon, singing, loudly, invented nonsense syllables in no known language, to pop tunes on the radio like "Al Di La." The permission granted to children.

But why should *writing* constitute such a betrayal? Summoning Senhor Valter, Dona Judite, Mort the Sport in writing further opens out that far, that long, this ever-widening distance. Both ways: my six-page letter to Senhor Valter; Dona Judite's endlessly cheerful letters to me; and now, here, this new violation. For this is what words do, isn't it?

That's why fishing with Tardelli always felt, always feels, better than *Fishing With Tardelli*. I thought language and memory could stand in, again, for experience. Well, they can, they do. Don't they?

Who decided on this nomenclature, Par, is unknown. My father moved some time soon after 1956, as I later discovered, into an unknown house and household in Montreal with the two other little boys, Lawrence and Philip, the boys Derek and I had met over ginger ale in our dim Sherbrooke Street apartment on that summer Sunday afternoon before we'd gone to Brazil. My mother's new husband, those Montreal little boys' first father — Unca — began to live in 1956 with us, his two new little boys, in Rio.

This, now, we all know. We know names, we know a few dates. This is worse than knowing nothing.

I knew my father in Montreal for a few moments before I turned seven. *Here's the facts, ma'am, just the facts: My name's Jack Webb; I'm a cop.* My parents got divorced in Montreal when I was two, my mother remarried when I was six, and we moved to Brazil.

My father came to Brazil to visit us in 1957, when we were still living in Copacabana. He stayed nearby at the

Copacabana Palace. He came to dinner at the penthouse on Miguel Lemos; he sat at the head of the table, one large hand on a soup spoon, his head bent. Senhor Valter and Dona Judite were overly polite and we boys were watchful. My father took us to the zoo in the north of the city, a long ride in the taxi he'd rented for the day. After some time on the grounds, he became ill there, but Derek and I wanted to see the lions before we left, and he permitted this.

Derek to me about our father, forty years ago: "Ele não chora." He doesn't cry, i.e., he doesn't complain. Derek rarely spoke Portuguese to me — unlike our mother, he did like the language, but selectively — but when he did, he said things that were true over time, until, for him, they weren't.

In Brazil we forgot most of our religion beneath another language and hid the remnants away. Until a few years later, when my grandparents north summoned each of us back, in turn, to become Bar Mitzvah, to "enter the ranks of Israel."

Montreal, August, 1962, three years before the *Ponta Negra*. The summer before four years of Jewish boarding school in Connecticut. I had just begun to fish with Tardelli. A month earlier I had gone out with him, Poporoca, Marilí, and Walter Gouveia for the first time on the *Moby Dick*, caught my first three bluefish. I remember the feeling of the first fish on my line. I was using a silver zigzag, zeegee-zagee in Portuguese, learning how to fish, puxa puxa; that first bluefish sends the sudden tight tension of its shaking weight coursing up the line into my hands, and I am there for life. Tá lá, it's there, I heard Tardelli mutter at his line. I was watching the men leaning over the water, all on one side of the boat. They were barefoot. Tá lá; they are there. I am there. Or I am here: Atwood, forever, "I want this. I want / this." The line we used most was linha sessenta, thin circumference, six-tenths of a millimetre, transparent nylon, although at times some of the Portuguese — Poporoca among them — favoured green linha setenta, seven-tenths, a touch thicker.

I am staying with my grandparents at 4332 Westmount Avenue, before we named it the Ponderosa. I am standing in the sunshine in the back driveway off Argyle. Summer 1962: I'm twelve. A white Buick Skylark convertible, its top down, blue interior, pulls in. At the wheel, I think, is my father. I am not certain. It's been a few years since I've seen him.

My father steps out of the car and I see that his eyes are blue. I am surprised. I thought they were brown, I tell him.

Years later, I learn to sing and play Crystal Gayle's *Don't It Make My Brown Eyes Blue*.

The internal grand inquisitor waxes contemptuous at these shallow equivalencies. *So what? Pop songstress lyrics, long-tressed dewy-eyed few-hit wonder, and you make a connection to what you saw in your little world when you were twelve in your grandparents' driveway, your father's blue eyes? Why don't you write Crystal Gayle and tell her? She'll be thrilled.*

Lyrics and literature and life. Choose your categories and your integuments with care. Do not divagate. Do not confound one category with another.

That night my father takes me to Ruby Foo's for dinner with his wife, the other Judith. For reasons unknown, she is silent and sorrowing.

I'd become aware, maybe in Brazil, that they had married at some indeterminate time in Montreal. Why would I not remember *when*, *where* I'd learned this part of the saga?

The Saturday evening after my Bar Mitzvah that morning, early November 1962, my father takes Derek and me, Lawrence and Philip and their mother to dinner, to celebrate, in the Beaver Room at the Queen Elizabeth Hotel. At the Ponderosa Dona Judite offers, on our way out the door into the chilled air, "He has to show everyone he's a big shot, doesn't he."

At dinner in the Beaver Room the backs of my legs behind my knees seize up and lock, I can't move. My father helps me up out of the chair, walks me out of the dining room and back in.

These little episodes last five or six years, then dissipate; I learn to counteract them with a ritual flexing of groups of muscles to a syncopated rhythm, beginning at my toes and heels, then the knees, the hips, once at the groin, fingers, then biceps, shoulders, and ending with one blink of the eyes. Then in reverse. To assure myself that I am in place. That I am. And that *I got rhythm*.

During this time just before my Bar Mitzvah in Montreal, Dona Judite, up from Brazil, takes us once to meet my father for lunch at a restaurant downtown. Looking over the menu, she tells us, briskly, to "order something expensive," points to the lamb chops. For an instant this is lost on me, but I ask for the lamb chops. Derek too.

Although I saw my father intermittently in the years between 1962 and 1970 — I knew where he was, and for most of the time he knew where I was — it was only when I was twenty and returned to Montreal for a few years before leaving again that I began to form a connection with him. He died when I was in my mid-forties so that I had roughly twenty-five years of knowing him in the flesh, and since for over twenty of those years I lived in other places, that does not now seem like a lot of time in a life.

Perhaps that is why memory *insists* — to make up for lost time. Why *lost time* calls immediately to metaphor, why *making up for lost time* becomes so fraught, why words, phrases refuse to remain literal. The affair with words, it never ends.

By the time I'd returned from LA to Montreal in the fall of 1969 at twenty, memory's arc had begun to unmoor itself, had begun to waver between time and space, *down*

south to Rio, *up* north to Montreal. And then in North America, *west* to LA for four years, *east* to Montreal for three, *west* again, this time to Western Canada for four decades, *east* again, to Toronto. Until time became a place. Until vines of language entwined around each other, more ivy, kin to the vines climbing the back of my grandparents' house on Argyle.

To myself I clothed my hallucinated return to Montreal from LA in mystical robes.

I left LA suddenly one evening in my car, on the road, headed to the airport. I handed some money to two surprised Black dudes at a restaurant counter, then decided I'd drive to Montreal, not fly, and drive via Vegas to cleanse myself of my father's gambling addiction. I made it as far as Barstow, California, before abandoning the car because I decided it was tainted with Senhor Valter's influence. I hitched into town, kicked off the highway twice by two cops in the same patrol car, the second time less friendly, through a bullhorn. That night I climbed a hill, a rattlesnake clattered at my feet, I conversed with God, a hot and low star entered my chest. I rode the Greyhound back to LA. Derek met me at the airport. When we arrived in Montreal I told him, told my father who had come to meet us, *no press.*

That evening I stand raving in my father's living room. I tell him I've left USC because it is irrelevant, because I can write any examination they give me, because I know more and differently. Because I wrote, "Impatience," I explain to him, on the Reason for Withdrawal form I was asked to complete.

His blue eyes are filled as he listens to me. I wish to explain to Dona Judite the next day, at the Ponderosa, why Henry Miller's essays are so important, and I am excited at the prospect; I have a speech ready about Miller's title, *The Wisdom of the Heart*. Phrases from the essays arise at the ready, then and now: about Goethe, Miller advises, "Everything nourished him." Yes! I exclaim to myself. But in my father's living room it isn't literature but life, more directly, that I wish to address.

I was readying another lecture for my mother the next day on Keats's letter about negative capability; in LA it had put me in a fever, it had inspired me. I was certain that Keats was referring to me, to my ability to hold mental conflict at bay and to focus, relentless, on ambiguity. In LA I had imbibed the Romantics that year; I imagined the writing in a wine-coloured anthology, Blake, Byron, Wordsworth, above all Keats, as honey on the forehead. I wished to explain all of this to Dona Judite. I knew I could make it all clear.

"Do yourself a favour, Neil, stop thinking," she said to me. Before I could get to my lectures on Keats, Miller, Goethe.

My mother's brother David arrives at my father's house the next morning to drive me around the corner to the Ponderosa; I am not trusted to take the five-minute walk there alone. It is feared that I will wander off. I bring my guitar as ammunition, but it remains in its case. Many years later I learn that Mort the Sport attended a family meeting that afternoon to which I was not invited.

That night I take his car for a contemplative drive, but I get lost in Montreal East and pull into a police station, inform them in infirm French that I have important work to do. One of the officers has kind brown eyes, I note, that water like my father's blue ones. The officer is gentle with me in my mania. My father and a stepbrother come down to the station and we drive home in the two cars.

The next day I walk down the south side of Sherbrooke in exalted delirium. I believe that passersby are reaching out to me to be saved. I grant them salvation.

Thus begins my three-year interlude in Montreal.

Par in Montreal had other nicknames, most fondly, as we boys grew into our late teens and early twenties, Mort the Sport. Mort the Sport was a pathological gambler, addicted to betting on professional and college football, on Major League Baseball — his favourite — and hockey. He was addicted to card games — gin, blackjack, pinochle, and, at the casinos in Vegas and later, in Atlantic City, baccarat. He liked to drop in, unannounced, to the back rooms of the pawn shops on Saint Antoine Street East in Montreal to play a few hands of gin with the owner. Weekdays, late afternoon, he liked to stop in at the Linton Club on Guy Street to play pinochle for an hour or two on his way home.

When I was at USC in LA, he would call me in the fall before the weekend's games: "Who do you like, boy, USC or UCLA?" Or, "How are you fixed for blades?" Sometimes I didn't understand the argot. When I bought a VW Beetle in the summer of 1970 in Montreal, on its maiden voyage he asked me to give him a lift downtown; lowering himself into the front seat, he asked me, "How's the pickup in this, boy?" I explained that it was a four-cylinder, it wasn't very quick. "No, no, boy, I'm asking, how's the pickup in this thing?" Eyeing me sidelong.

Or, two decades later in Florida, where he wintered in his last years, he'd explain to me that his son Jonathan's astuteness was well thought of at the track, "His opinion is respected," nodding, quietly proud. But he didn't know what to do about the threats he got over the telephone about Jon. Driving around Montreal with me at the wheel, one of his favourite pastimes, going around his parking lots — "Take a right stash here, boy, do a hesitation waltz in this alley. Watch the rubbydub lying in front of the garage door." — he'd ask me, "What should I do? They say they're going to break this, they're going to break that unless they get the money he owes them in forty-eight hours."

Having no advice for him, I become sanctimonious. I lecture him. He falls silent. Nearing the house on Clarke in the evening, the rounds finished, he'd tell me, "Don't pull in, boy, turn around, let's go downtown again," and ask me to drive far east along Sherbrooke, buy some time. "You have to know French well now to do business here, boy. If you're coming into business with me, your French has to be better, you understand me?"

His gambling overlaid his life. When the new technique of counting cards in blackjack appeared on the scene, he bought the book, sat us four boys down with him in the den upstairs, and explained it to us. We would learn the technique and the five of us would fly to Vegas, he told us, try it on for size. We were game, but it didn't happen. The Vegas casinos had got wise, had begun to watch for card counters.

He smoked endlessly, Du Mauriers, punctuated with cigars, Coronas. He ambled; he was deliberate. He compiled elaborate statistics on starting pitchers, odds, ERA's, all of these figures entered neatly and methodically on the pads of the large lined sheets more properly used for their designated purpose, to record licence plates, show daily balances on the lots that comprised his parking business. He entered the figures with the thin gold-plated ballpoint pen that my sister Marilyn and I bought him for his birthday one year. He lunched regularly with his bookie, Harry Goodman, an affable man, at the Brioche Room in the Mount Royal Hotel. He liked his nickname; he liked it when we asked him: "Morton, how's the Sportin'?"

Early one summer evening in 1970 the cops pulled up to the house on Clarke and two young guys got out, came politely to the door, asked my father to come downtown with them. "Fellas, why don't I follow you in my car," he suggested, but they demurred. He sent me up to his bedroom to retrieve his sports jacket, but I missed his signal and failed to remove the little book from the inside pocket. The officers exulted. My father's two little boys from his second marriage glowered at them. His wife was annoyed with me.

These were the years when we four boys from the first two marriages would assemble in Montreal for the summer to work on his parking lots, driving in from LA, from Miami, from London, Ontario, from Allentown, PA. Before dispersing again in the fall. We lived with him in his house on the corner of Clarke and Hudson, with his wife, the second Judith, and the three children from his second marriage. First, second — that depends on the storyteller.

Mort the Sport's tastes in music ran to old-style soft shoe, to intimations of gangsters in alleyways — as in "Mack the Knife." Or, in another, more sentimental vein, he would ask one of us to sing: "Oh my papa / To me he was so wonderful / Oh my papa / To me he was so good." He had to say the words; he was spectacularly tone-deaf. The only man who matched him in this regard was Senhor Valter, as Senhor Valter cheerfully acknowledged. While Tardelli, head thrown back, declaimed opera in fake Spanish, in false Italian. A few lines of "Granada," gorgeously full-throated, theatrical.

Mort the Sport's favourite writer, no surprise: Damon Runyon. *Harry the Horse* and his pals in New York. The lingo. I bought him a Runyon collection, *From First to Last*;

for some reason two copies remain with me. In the back of one, Mort the Sport's careful calculations in ballpoint, circa 1985: he is explaining to me how in fifteen years, "you'll be on easy street." Reading his figures now I think of A.M. Klein's great poem "Heirloom," in which Klein, reading one night, discovers a white hair from his father's beard. My father's voice, the measured syllables.

In the mid-seventies he decided to give his five children 20 percent each of his company, a legal manoeuvre. He assembled us in his office, gave us each a thick folded-over document prepared by his accountant. Explained its import.

Derek threw his copy across the room at me. "Você viu isso?" Have you seen this? A rhetorical question posed in a language only he and I understood. To accompany the dismissive flinging of the document.

My father stared at him in surprise. Silence. The discussion proceeded.

Thus did that father, that son evolve. If Derek were to tell this story, it would be very different. A different *narrative*: when the postmodernists arrived, long ago now, they taught the culture at large how fluid the term could become, and drained it. The watchword now of presidents and politicians, bankers and CEOs. Never mind; our *narratives* began to diverge. So that by the time Mort the Sport lay dying in the early nineties, Derek asked him in the hospital, "Dad, who are you?" This was reported to me with disapproval. But I see it differently. I have a different *narrative*. For Derek, my father had become unknowable. Period. It was urgent for Derek to *know*.

Montreal's Expo Summer, 1967. The Canadian dollar was worth five cents less than the American one but we took the tourists' bucks at par. We thought we were slick. Back in the main office, tenth floor of the Gordon Brown Building fronting on Burnside, in the process of becoming de Maisonneuve, we gave the collected American dollars to my father's older brother Aaron, the alleged racketeer (we called him Uncle Moneybags in those days — he chuckled, he didn't mind; unlike the Cohens, none of the Besners minded a nickname). He gave us Canadian currency plus five cents per dollar, in exchange. We pocketed the profit.

At the back of the Gordon Brown Building, furriers mingled with Chassids. When I first saw these men, at twelve, I understood that they were Jewish, but they seemed to be of a different race from the Westmount Jews, who themselves lived in tiers. The Besners seemed then to me to be street smart, and the Cohens — my mother's parents — minor nobility.

Although it flourished under several names, we knew my father's business as Safeway Parking. We worked with many of the French Canadian men on the lots. We told each other their stories, inflected with our clumsy imitations of their English: "Speak da man, park da wall. For what you don' charge 'im doobleh?"

What they thought of our bad French remains unknown.

André Gagnon on St. Francis Xavier. Maurice Hebert, various lots. Fernande Houde on the big EZ. Claude Gagnon at the Mountain Street garage. The Molloy kid on Craig Street West. Old man Hekkola at nights in the garage on Mansfield. Maurice LaPlante, checker, brother in law of Roland Hebert, head checker, younger brother of Maurice, partner of Linda in the office. Where Mrs. (Grace) Bullock and Helen Story and Robbie held down the fort for my father, who came in for an hour or two every morning before leaving to make his rounds of the lots, before following up on the day's action, the day's odds, on the telephone.

Wolf Bronet, Holocaust survivor, marathon runner, head of the legendary Wolf Pack, presiding in the office, spoke to his wife Henya every day at noon on the phone. "Do you balance, Neil?" We kidded each other about the daily envelopes with cash from each lot; I drew stick figures on them, balancing. "You have to balance."

Rocky Vito, a supervisor, cocky, sharp dresser, black shoes sparkling, who got permanently *ventilated* one day. Roland was held up, one of we four brothers too. "Don' fock aroun', giv 'im da cash," Roland advised me, but it never happened. "You 'ongry, tabarnak," he remarked to me watching me watch a woman in a bar after work. He told me his favourite time of day was early morning driving to work, the quiet, the empty streets. "No fockin' noise." His older brother Maurice teased me, "Na, na na na, perdu dans Montréal," he sang to me, laughing.

One day I added a quarter to André Gagnon's tip box in his shack on St. Francis Xavier when he was out on the lot and I was working there with him. I never told him or anyone else. Twenty-five cents of absolution, an incremental instalment plan. Like the American cash I spontaneously doled out at the airport in LA.

A grey worn down Sunday on the little EZ, St. Alexandre Street, no business, "Bridge Over Troubled Water" playing on my transistor. I am inexplicably crying, and a memory arises, on the pavement in Montreal, of a grey drizzly day on the water near Cotunduba in the bay in Rio, a Sunday afternoon, no fish, Senhor Valter and Tardelli on a far planet next to me. These bleaknesses touch each other as in a dream, out of time. They are pre-departure bleaknesses, auguries.

In the basement of my father's house on the corner of Clarke Avenue and Hudson, we watched him play gin with his buddies. Pink fifty-dollar bills were exchanged; one came to several of us on a snowy night for pushing his friend Lawrence Yanofsky's Cadillac out of the deep snow. We were rich.

In those three years in Montreal I often ate lunch with my father. We walked north from the Gordon Brown Building across the Big Atlas lot, as we knew it, before the City expropriated it to make way for President Kennedy Avenue running west from Bleury, kicking off what became an eleven-year court battle. We ate at Nathan's, a little deli. There I told him one day that I was floundering. "Now is the time to flounder, boy."

When the lawsuit was over and he had won, he sat across from me at Murray's, a restaurant he favoured near the northwest corner of Sherbrooke and Claremont. Early evening. "Was it worth it, boy?" he asked me. His arm laid across the booth behind him. The answer was evident. The City made him and his companies a target from then on.

He took his own quiet satisfaction in my studying literature. When Saul Bellow visited Montreal in the later seventies, over my protestations my father had a copy of my master's thesis delivered to Bellow at his hotel. When my first book was published in 1988, he bought twenty-five copies and had them delivered to his siblings, to his family. He took me to lunch with one of his bankers at the RBC branch across the street from the office, a short stocky woman, mitteleuropean accent, sharp brown eyes behind thick lenses. He had me give her my thesis on Bellow. "You are committing spiritual suicide in Western Canada," she told me. This gave me pause.

In the early seventies, Mort the Sport wished me to come into business with him. Each Friday for two years I worked at Safeway, a day off from Honours English at McGill. I came into the office at Gordon Brown in the morning to prepare the week's deposits, walk them down to the Bank of Montreal on the corner of Bleury and St. Catherine. At the bank they gave me a little room at the back, a calculator, rubber bands. Coco the bank teller, short stocky blonde with a big laugh, snickered with me when Rusty Staub, Le Grand Orange, walked in. (When my mother's father took me some years earlier to his barber for a haircut, Mr. Tousingnant asked me who number 28 was for the Alouettes. It was George Dixon, I told him.)

How could I have known that of the two parents at home, south and north, my father would remain most alive to me? My sister Marilyn, his first child from his second marriage, would say to me in the months after his death in 1994, "Sometimes I can almost touch him, he's almost there."

I never spoke of Tardelli to him. I don't think he ever heard the name or knew who Tardelli was. He did know I liked to fish; at twenty-one, when at dusk I would drive out to Nun's Island and walk down in waders under the Champlain Bridge to spin for pike, or at nightfall for pickerel, doré — walleye in the West — he would come to visit, with his perpetual cigar, with his slow and careful and measured gait, watching from up on the gravel bank until the mosquitoes drove him away.

He was by then a heavy man, but very quick with figures in his head. Late in his life, he waved away the little machines his sons had begun to use to calculate percentages, twelve months' rent, net potential profits on a parcel of land after all expenses had been figured in. He could make the calculations more quickly in his head. In the early fifties, a refugee from his father's clothing business — not to be confused with my mother's father's clothing businesses, for the two establishments, like their progenitors, were very different — my father was the first operator of private parking lots in downtown Montreal, the first to conceive of the parking business as a real estate venture.

He never mentioned the divorce, never referred to my mother. When they were together at a social occasion, she was offhand, casual, charming. Or snide. At Derek's wedding in England in the summer of 1975, my father fell backwards off a low cushion and she laughed quietly but so that others could see. Derek and my mother believed him to be the "most socialized person" they knew. The mischaracterization intrigued me.

I never mentioned my father or Montreal to Tardelli because Canadian, American were useless distinctions to him. For Tardelli, Senhor Valter was my father and his boss, the patrão, Dona Judite the beautiful but severe patroa. Who, you will remember, referred to Tardelli as Lady Chatterley's Lover. To have tried to explain to Tardelli that my real father lived in Montreal, in Canada, would have been foolish. It brought to mind another of Tardelli's angry sermons at the yacht club, this one about fathers in Rio with children jogados como lixo por aí, thrown

126

away like garbage here and there. Not to be confused with his other half-proud dockside admission one evening that he had many children himself espalhados por aí, scattered here and there.

To have tried to explain to Tardelli about the first marriages, second marriages, the twinned names, would have been to invite frank disbelief.

When my father came to Rio again in August 1965, I was in Manaus on the *Ponta Negra*. I learned of his arrival by a telex given to me by Adão, the ship's radio man: Seu pai está aqui no Rio em busca de Philip, read the message from Senhor Valter; your father is here in Rio to bring Philip back — Senhor Valter's second son by his first marriage, come to Rio to live with us for several months at 126 Codajás for reasons unspecified. After conferring with Captain Serra, I decided to remain in Manaus. My father and his second Judy returned to Montreal with Philip. A few weeks later I returned to Rio and thence back to my last year of boarding school in Connecticut.

Between 1962 and 1994 I saw him sporadically. I saw him in Montreal for a few holidays from boarding school; a few summers, as I've said, I worked on his lots. Two or three times he came to LA en route to Vegas, where I drove out to join him for a day or two. I hung out at the two-dollar blackjack tables while he played high stakes baccarat. His face at the table white and beaded with sweat. A glass of ice water at his side.

We went to a Frank Sinatra show. He was no longer able to hit the high notes, he whistled. Two women picked me up in the bar at the Sands, took me to a house party. The next morning Mort the Sport told me, "If you were with the older one, that's no bargain." I was.

In an LA hotel corridor he challenged me:

"Knock, knock."

I asked who was there.

"It's hack."

I asked who that was.

"It's Hockey Night in Canada!"

A moment later he told me, still in the corridor, "The problem is that parents don't want to let go." The next morning by the pool he gave me a pack of Du Mauriers, said to me, "I don't have any answers." He was courteous to my girlfriend, Georgina Torres from Whittier, whose handsome Mexican father was also quietly polite with me.

He was courteous with all my girlfriends. "How is the party from Thunder Bay," he asked me in 1972 after she and I, together at McGill for our final year there, had broken up.

He came to Regina in 1974 when I graduated. He came to Vancouver in 1976 when, after Levesque had been elected, my father travelled across Canada, thinking about moving from Montreal. He didn't.

After his Regina visit, I published a poem about him in *The Fiddlehead* but he never saw it and by then I was in

Europe for a year. In Vancouver we played gin in his room at the Bayshore; if I won, $100 for books, if he won, $100 for salmon to take home with him. It took me decades to realize he'd let me win.

"Salt of the earth," he murmured to me after Sunday night dinner at my French Canadian girlfriend's parents' house in Regina in 1974. Jacqueline Toupin was from Montmartre, Saskatchewan. When we visited Rio for ten days over Christmas in 1973–74, Dona Judite put us in separate rooms although we lived together in Regina. Mort the Sport did the same in Montreal in the Summer of 1974 before we boarded a Greek freighter for Europe. "The children," he explained.

"I have never been so offended and hurt in my life," Dona Judite told me a year later in Montreal at the bar in the Ritz Carlton; she'd discovered our nightly visits to each other's bedroom in Rio, had not spoken with us for our last three days there. "Jacqueline," said Senhor Valter to my astonishment, quietly, from the head of the table at breakfast in Rio, January 2020, when I mentioned the episode, but not her name. "He gives me the willies," said Jacqui to me in Brazil, Christmas 1973. The three of us played Scrabble by the pool in the bright mid-morning heat: Senhor Valter offered the word *aformish*, assembling the tiles precisely to fall on the rich red triple score. Seven letters plus *a*. He reasoned, quietly cheerful with me in the heat, that this was a perfectly plausible word, shook his head in benign wonderment at my obstinacy. After a reasoned five-minute dispute, he withdrew it.

What does it mean that I can hear my father's voice fifty years later, hear the phrases in his tone, see the gestures, what he wore; that I remember the weather? That looking down now at my left hand at the dinner table, I see, I have seen for fifty years, that I took on his folding of the thumb over the index finger as he ate?

In Rio, I learned more consciously to flick the cigarette ashes, like Tardelli, with my forefinger.

I had three fathers, and they are all with me. It is always clear which father is most alive to me, how, and when, but it has nothing to do with who does, who does not draw breath.

Back at McGill from Winnipeg for a year in 2001–02, in a role colleagues in Winnipeg called "the Whiskey Fellowship"— the Seagram's Chair, the idea of which was to come to the East to talk about the Canadian West, terra incognita to many — more foreign in Montreal than New York, Boston, Philadelphia, less known and more exotic than anywhere in Europe — I discovered that in Montreal there was, had been for as many years as my father's immediate family, a clan of Besners I came to think of as "the shadow Besners," descended from a brother of my grandfather's, many of whom, in my father's generation, bore the same first names as their first cousins: Morty, Bernie, Aaron, and so forth.

My father had never mentioned this to me. When I called Dona Judite in Rio in the fall of 2001, she told me she'd never heard of them.

This took me aback. A sociologist at McGill specializing in the history of Jews in Canada, Morton Weinfeld, told me that this was a common story, the twinned names in the children of that generation of emigrants, but was silent on the families' dissociation. I called Esther, the widow of my father's next oldest brother, Bernie. She cheerfully confirmed that family's existence, suggested I contact my father's younger sister Queenie in Ottawa, the last one then remaining of the nine siblings, of Dona Judite's bewhiskered cartoon cats drawn at the table in the Winter Garden for Derek and me fifty years earlier. Queenie, as cheerfully as Esther and in more detail, told stories of those Besners, of going with them for ice cream. Rosanna, Esther's daughter, one of my legion of first cousins in Montreal, had me over for coffee a month before the coronavirus to meet Gail Besner, daughter of one of the shadow Besners, who lived in an apartment down the hall from her in the 4300 on De Maisonneuve.

How could this family have lived all these years in Montreal without my father — he who was so particular about family connections — ever having spoken of them? How could Dona Judite have never heard of them?

My father's namesake, Mortimer, or Morty, outlived my father by eight years. He died at eighty-five in June 2002, a month after I'd left McGill to drive back to Winnipeg.

His gravestone in the Tifereth Beth David Jerusalem Congregation Cemetery on Rue de la Savane closely resembles my father's in the Shaar Hashomayim Cemetery on Côte des Neiges. This Mortimer had a wife, Lily, three children, three grandchildren.

For all that he was so intent on me getting to know the Besners, my father could be comically absent-minded about names. He was intent in the later eighties on my coming to Montreal from Winnipeg for a family Bar Mitzvah. "It will be a nice occasion for you to get reacquainted with the family," he said to me on the phone. I agreed to come, asked him on the phone the name of the Bar Mitzvah boy. "Now you've got me," he said.

During that year in Montreal, 2001–02, mine was the only car I saw with a Manitoba plate. On our way to Kenosie, Saskatchewan, camping with Jacqui Toupin in '74 — we spent a day in our tent in pounding rain, then hail; I read *Tess of the D'urbervilles* — a Mountie pulled us over on the highway, asked me about the Quebec plates on my VW. More lonely than an alien, west or east. The Mountie searched the car thoroughly, friendly, musing, "Everything from soup to nuts."

My father liked to tell me stories about his father, Joseph Alter, J.A. Besner, who, as a teenager, my father told me, peddled eyeglasses in a horse-drawn cart near Montreal.

Who had my father's blue eyes, but more shrewd, glinting with more light. Who as a young teenager had left Poland and his mother when she was widowed and remarried and he did not like his new stepfather. Who had gone to the World's Fair in Paris in 1900 before taking ship to Montreal. Whom Mama Besner, Mort the Sport's mother, had spotted disembarking and said, "That one's for me," my father liked to tell me. Who later came to be known as The Judge because, my father told me, he dispensed advice to those who came to him on the Main. Who founded J.A. Besner's, the clothing firm, where my father worked briefly before founding his parking business. Who, when he was eighty-five, gave each of his many grandchildren a thousand dollars. Who bet the greyhounds in the winter at the track in Florida. Who, the stories ran later, could not keep any nurse for very long when he was old and alone, when in the evenings his sons took turns going to his apartment on Kensington, within walking distance of the shul, to play pinochle with him, because he was too fond of these women and he patted them too persistently.

Why, in his storytelling mode, would Mort the Sport never have mentioned his namesake in that shadow family?

If we were in Montreal or nearby when his mother died in the early sixties, or when a sibling of his died, he brought Derek and me to town for the funeral.

"There is nothing wrong with tenderness," he said to me one evening upstairs in the den of his house on Clarke, shortly after I'd returned to Montreal from LA.

When he went in for his last operation at the Vic in Montreal, I told him on the phone, "I love you."

"Me too," he said, afraid.

When J.A. died at ninety in the summer of 1970, my father had me drive him downtown to Peel and Sainte-Catherine that night to pick up the *Gazette* so that he could read the obituary. We sat together in the dark car.

"Boy, you should visit your grandparents more often, they're getting old," he often told me in those years, referring to my mother's parents in the Ponderosa. Referring to himself. Beginning in the seventies, he would repeat softly to himself through me, "Getting old, boy, getting old." Or, more defiantly but in the same mode, exiting from the car on a summer evening, Expo summer, to we four boys playing football on Hudson in the street: "Let me see that ball, boys," punting it to us. Ambling into the house.

On a weekend summer afternoon a few years before he died, I was in Montreal, visiting. He was relaxing on his bed with a Du Maurier, ruminating.

"You know, boy, this family has a lot of history. A lot of history."

Silence.

"What would you say, boy, to the following." Another pause. A drag on the Du Maurier.

"What if I made it worth your while to write the family history? I'll talk to my brothers and to Queenie, I'll get them to participate, you can tape them. Otherwise," he paused, "it'll all be forgotten." He paused. "What do you say?"

I was thinking of Senhor Valter, of a drizzly afternoon a year earlier at the big house in Rio, sitting with him under the eave by the pool to stay dry. A gentle and misting rain. He'd said to me "I have so many memories of all these years in Brazil, the growth of the businesses, and they are all going to be lost."

Senhor Valter was singularly incapable of telling a story: the details distracted him endlessly, led him down endlessly branching sidestreets of asides, of clarification, revision, explication. It was fascinating. It was maddening. Senhor Valter, with that magnificently elaborated mind, was incapable of telling a story. Of narration.

I mumbled something pleasantly incoherent to my father. I am surprised to discover that my memory fails me: I can't recall what I said. But the import was "no, I won't." And, silently, "I won't come into business with you. No," although in the world, gently, I sidled away. For forty years I sidled away from my father, I strode away from Senhor Valter.

Senhor Valter came frequently to Montreal in those latter years with his partner Rochelle. Frequently, they were guests at Clarke Avenue, then at the apartment on Mountain Street, for Friday night dinners, for Sunday brunches.

"He's an odd duck," my father said to me of Senhor Valter, "always underfoot."

"He's my great friend," Senhor Valter said to me of my father.

Of course when Mort the Sport died in 1994, Walter flew up for the funeral. After I spoke at the funeral at Paperman's, Senhor Valter grabbed me from behind, his arms encircling me, whispered loudly, "That was fabulous and fantastic." Dona Judite on the phone from Rio, marvelling, "Who knew Morty was such an alte kaker, seven years older than me?"

CODA

We met forty-nine years ago in an honours seminar on William Blake, Winter 1971, her third year at McGill, my first. I'd returned to Montreal from LA and three years at USC.

She was from Thunder Bay. She left there at sixteen, vowing never to return. She has kept her vow.

That summer after the Blake seminar, June of '71, we came across each other in sunshine, a bright but cool weekday morning on Pine Avenue. She was carrying a brown bag of groceries.

"I'll buy you breakfast if you carry this to my place," she said. I noted the odd phrasing, and I carried the paper bag.

We'd had eyes for each other since the Blake seminar. We played tennis once or twice that June. I noted that she was awkward but cheerful on the court. As if this activity were a preliminary rite in which she dutifully participated.

In July I went to Brazil for a month. When I got back at the end of August, we began to see each other in earnest.

In earnest means that we began to have sex nearly every day that fall.

She went to Thunder Bay for Christmas. In the winter and into the spring we continued to have unbridled sex. The men on my father's lots told me, laughing, that I was looking pale.

We do not remember conversations from this time. We didn't know what conversation meant. Looking back, I think of Garnet French and Del Jordan in *Lives of Girls and Women*.

But Garnet French, Del Jordan are characters in a novel. You must choose your integuments with care while you try to find a way to imagine fifty years.

I try to conceive of this missing time as an arc, as half a circle. I try to imagine its curve west and then back east, arching across North America. Its sister arc pulses *north* and *south* and *north*, a metronome softly singing. When I take Gail to Brazil now, the metronome lulls us, pulls us, lulls.

On principle, I did not attend graduation from McGill in June of 1972. On principle I flew to Ireland to begin a year's sojourn in Europe, but I returned to Montreal ten days later.

In Ireland I fished. I drank Guinness. I flirted at pubs with friendly women. I hitchhiked around the south. Eventually I stood at a dock in Cork, watching a raggy group of kids playing soccer on the cobblestones next to a small freighter. I can hear their accents.

Thinking of the *Ponta Negra*, I thought to board the freighter and ask for work. Instead, I took the bus to Shannon and flew back to Montreal the next day.

I had not yet read *Ultramarine*. But it wouldn't have mattered then. I wouldn't have been able to distinguish the categories, literature and life. I still can't.

Can you? Have you decided why you're reading, have you decided how to read? Do you remember? Do you remember "Funes the Memorious"?

The first day back in Montreal from Ireland, early July 1972, I walked into the ghetto to visit my friend Ian Walker, with whom I had split the Lionel Shapiro Prize for Creative Writing at McGill a few months earlier, $400 each. We got drunk then in his second-floor walk-up. He climbed out onto the rooftop under his balcony, squatting in the cool sunlight of a spring afternoon, mad green eyes glaring in defiance. Back on his heels, against what?

Now, back from Ireland, I looked at the sky again, roof-level, from his balcony. I saw a cloud shaped like Australia and made it into the first lines of a song:

> There's a cloud shaped like Australia
> Moving toward the sun
> If that's the way that free things go
> The afternoon's undone
> While the sparrows freak the trees
> My thoughts run dying on the breeze
> Makes my mind such a fast disease
> I can't stop now won't you push me please
> I can't stop now, like a cloud, I'm on the run.

For decades I alternately sang the song and critiqued it. What cloud known to man is on the run? Later verses invoked Jesus, provoked uneasy glances in coffee houses east and west. Song lyrics, street lyrics. Clouds in writing, clouds above. Saul Bellow, Joni Mitchell.

In those years in the early to mid-seventies, back from Regina on visits, I could still walk down Sainte-Catherine and see people I'd known at McGill. One day I ran into Ian. He squinted and then nodded at me. He told me he was working for *Reader's Digest*. Neither of us wished to talk.

For decades I wondered what became of him. He was the most talented writer I knew then. Mad green eyes on the roof.

My $400 was for a piece entitled "Ocean Days," a mawkish prototype, I realized many years later, for the opening of *Fishing With Tardelli*. On the flight to Ireland in 1972 — the return ticket, Air Canada, cost me $180 — I fumbled with the pages in my lap. The Tardelli figure was named Severiano.

I had hired an older lady in Côte des Neiges to type the piece for the McGill contest. She had me sit down at her typewriter in her kitchen and type in "fuck" where it occurred twice. She told me that she would not type the word herself. For the manuscript's "long wide thick body," describing the big bluefish Tardelli's predecessor, Tardelli's successor Severiano had caught on a summer day in July at Imbuí, Brazilian midwinter, she had mistyped "wise" for wide. I liked the emendation. I let it stand.

Tardelli was alive then. He was younger then than I am now. His photographs then were secondary.

I have the piece Ian Walker wrote for the competition. It was an excerpt from a novel. It was brilliant. It featured a relationship between a first-person narrator, unnamed, and a young woman, Cordé. It was then the best thing I'd read by someone I knew.

I have never heard what became of Ian, of Cordé.

In the Spring of 1972 at Ian's, before I went to Ireland, Mort the Sport's "party from Thunder Bay" — Gail — was with me.

She appeared to me again in July of 1972, in the third verse of "A Cloud Shaped Like Australia":

> You ask me why I'm leaving,
> And when I cannot tell

We act like perfect strangers
And wish each other well.

What does it mean that she was now in a song, for all time?

She had come to Montreal in July to visit for a few days and I broke up with her. I drove her to the airport and came back to the apartment where I was living, on Stanley Street north of Sherbrooke, and watched my face in the mirror, crying.

That September I drove west to Regina to begin graduate school. They'd offered me $2200 for a teaching assistantship. At lunch with Mort the Sport that August, he told me, "If I were you, boy, I'd go." This was when he asked me about "the party from Thunder Bay."

Gail did not walk then; she strode. She did not think about the past, and she told me so.

While I worked at Safeway Parking on Fridays, our last year at McGill, she worked at the Sonesta Hotel on the northeast corner of Sherbrooke and Peel. Home turf for Vito Rizutto.

In the sixties all the sailors, the marinheiros at the yacht club, knew Tardelli and they all used his last name; as I have explained, he was the only one who had no nickname. "Tardelli, me dá 25 litros"; give me 25 litres from your boss's boat. Honour among thieves, as Senhor Valter had put it, Unca in those days.

Chi-Chico was from Cabo Frio, just up the coast from Rio. He came fishing with us a lot, although not as much as Poporoca or his fellow faux marinheiros from Portugal, Porquinho, piglet, said with affection, or taciturn Bacalhau, dried cod, said with respect. Bacalhau outlived all the marinheiros; I last saw him walking by me in the late nineties. He didn't recognize me. I didn't stop him. I never learned his real name, nor Poporoca's, Chi-Chico's, Porquinho's. Cabo Verde's at the fish store. Names, nicknames, meant differently then. Even, especially, Tardelli's name.

Chi-Chico was tall and lanky and when he threw out his lure his arm made a wide sweep and his line sailed in a high slowing arc before settling into the water. One afternoon at Ilha dos Pais we came upon a school of fish on top of the water. "Olha o peixe em cima," look at the fish on top, he said to Tardelli, "com o canoeiro no meio deles," with a canoe fisherman in the middle of them. He watched me, amused to see my expression change when I suddenly had a fish on. The noisy school of fish beating the water white. "Tá grosso," murmured Tardelli, it's thick. They are thick. They're teeming. The bite is on. No translation works. But one must try.

"Ele só quer saber do seus treze peixes," Poporoca grunts, he only cares about his thirteen fish. We're at Ilha dos Pais again, in warm sunshine in the early afternoon. I'm fourteen.

Before I begin watching the riddling waves unfurling over each other on the beach at Ipanema, in Leblon.

I have no memory of Tardelli ever calling me by name, ever saying my name. He must have.

Tardelli, Chi-Chico, and I are out on a sullen winter afternoon in hazy sheets of warm rain, in a moderate *sudoeste*, the southwest wind that brings bad weather. We are on the *Judite*, 29 feet, the first of two boats Senhor Valter named after my mother (unsubtly, he named his next boat *Joana*, after his daughter). Thick grey sky, clouds massed at eye level, rain, the boat pitching. Tardelli and Chi-Chico go down below for a nap. I'm fifteen. In a month this will be the summer of the *Ponta Negra*. Alone up top at the helm I feel brave, I feel like a *marinheiro*. Entrusted with the well-being of the two men below. For forty minutes I am like them.

That Brazilian winter, in my small boat with Tardelli, early evening, we stalled beyond the buoy of the Magdalena in the middle of the bay. He could not restart the engine. The tide was ebbing and we were drifting out to sea. No ships or boats, no canoes in sight.

I helped him take off the heavy motor mount. The Ford truck motor exposed, painted marine blue. O Fordeco, he'd dubbed it. The Ford guy. Now it lay stilled. It wouldn't turn over.

Tardelli bends over it with a screwdriver, fingering rubber lines near the carburetor, tells me to turn on the ignition. Trying to see if gas is getting to the engine. Ten minutes, fifteen minutes. We are drifting. I say something

144

inane. What did I say? He looks up at me and shakes his head, "Não é engraçado, meu filho." It's not funny, kid. "Meu filho," my son, literally, but in Brazil most often used on the street as "kid." Tardelli's tone takes me aback. He is serious. Five minutes later he gets the engine started but he remains grave for another moment as we turn to head back in gathering darkness.

Chi-Chico and Tardelli have a competition one morning to see who can strip the varnish more efficiently from the two motor mounts on Chi-Chico's boss's boat. Five or six of us egg them on. Tardelli favours quick swabs of turpentine and short scrapes; Chi-Chico, a more deliberate rhythm with longer swaths. Chi-Chico finishes first. Tardelli congratulates him. Then the sanding, the revarnishing. The conversation migrates to how one learns about things, how one knows things. We all listen to Tardelli declaim. Why is he the acknowledged orator at these gatherings? He quizzes one marinheiro, rhetorically: "Você é dono de uma fábrica de sapato?" Do you own a shoe factory? "Então como é que você sabe tanto de sapatos?" So how come you know so much about shoes? Everyone laughs. "Fala, Tardelli." Speak, Tardelli, runs the literal falsification, worse than a lie. Tell it like it is. It's what it is. Different kinds of lies.

What would Tardelli think if he knew I'd named my boat after him? That I'd written about him? Would he be insulted, offended?

He laughs.

On the dock, looking across the water at the flickering lights in the dark downtown, flicking an ash from his unfiltered Continental, he repeats, for all time, "Você é jovem, tem muito a aprender." You're young, you have a lot to learn.

What has writing to do with time, with living and being in time? Language, being, time: that unholy trinity. A cross to bear, to drag on the long Via Dolorosa. Literature and life.

I taught "Cloud Like Australia" to my son Dan in Winnipeg when he was twenty; I played it for Gail in 2017. Dan played it at a party there on my seventieth.

I told my son what it had to do with Gail. He laughed, she laughed. Language, being, time.

We'd met again in the spring of 2016. We'd known nothing of each other's lives in the intervening forty-five years. This is rare in Canada in our circles. You'd think we would have had to go out of our way to forget each other. That this required an act of will.

But no, "The art of losing isn't hard to master."

She was a widow; her Jewish husband Neil had died in 2011 after a long illness. She had two sons, I had a son and a daughter, all roughly the same age. I'd been married twice.

We got married in Vancouver in the late summer of 2017. Her apartment roommate from McGill, now a judge, presided. That fall, I moved to Toronto, having lived in the west since 1972.

Over time, as they say, can people change? Is there some essence, some core, that remains immutable? There are times when I will glance at her and see an expression redolent — more immediately than the word suggests — of 1971.

What's the relation between a look, a phrase, a way of walking — she still strides — and the person indwelling?

What's the relation between a person and a person in a song?

Sometimes it seems that memory wants to murder time and that writing wants to murder the imagination.

To remember everything is a fatal if involuntary compulsion. Worse might be to remember in words. My own private pandemic.

The doctors haven't found a vaccine for this one yet. But if they did, I don't know that I'd take it.

Imagine time thinking. On our long pandemic walks down Yonge Street, to Bloor, then a short way west down to Philosopher's Walk, where we stop at a bench on the right, the one with the plaque that excerpts from Elizabeth Bishop's great poem "The Moose."

We walk in the ravines. Or up Yonge to Heath, thence west to Avenue Road, and then south and east again down through the U of T campus. Or in the ravine up by Sunnybrook Hospital.

On Philosopher's Walk over the last two years, there has often appeared an older, slower black squirrel with grey and lighter grey patches. He is known there, but as far as we know, no one has named him.

We are trying to make up for lost time.

ACKNOWLEDGEMENTS

I would like to thank the entire team at ECW Press for their exemplary care and professionalism with this book. Publisher Jack David gave me, generously and unstintingly, timely support and astute advice from the very beginning — tempered with timely and wry asides. His colleagues — managing editor Sammy Chin, director of publicity and marketing Susannah Ames, publicists Elham Ali and Emily Varsava, digital and art director Jessica Albert, cover designer Sophie Paas, copy editor Jen Albert, language reader Rachel Morgenstern-Clarren, communications coordinator Michela Prefontaine, typesetter Jennifer Gallinger, and proofreader Shannon Parr — were, to a person, indefatigable and cheerfully efficient from first to last. I know there are many others at ECW who made invaluable contributions as well. My thanks to you all.

I am especially grateful to writer and editor Emily Schultz. Her generosity in offering her formidable talent and expertise to me was an inspiration.

To the late Andris Taskans and to Marjorie Poor at *Prairie Fire*: my thanks to you both for your patience and advice as you helped me to reshape several inchoate early versions into what eventually became the first chapter of this book.

To Brian Henderson, Catherine Hunter, and Steven Lewis: my great thanks to you for your careful and astute readings and re-readings of early drafts of the book, for your candour, your encouragement, and your enduring friendship.

Ao Manuel Tardelli, meu pai Brasileiro: sou eternamente grato.

To my family near and far, with us and departed: let us remember.

First and last, I owe more than I can tell to my wife Gail, who read innumerable drafts, day and night, dusk and dawn, and at all times spoke to me from her heart.

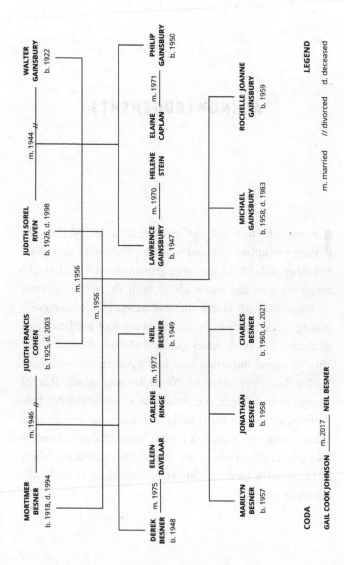

MORTIMER BESNER
b. 1918, d. 1994

m. 1946 //

JUDITH FRANCIS COHEN
b. 1925, d. 2003

m. 1956

JUDITH SOREL RIVEN
b. 1926, d. 1998

m. 1956

WALTER GAINSBURY
b. 1922

m. 1944 //

EILEEN DAVELAAR

m. 1975

DEREK BESNER
b. 1948

CARLENE RINGE

m. 1977

NEIL BESNER
b. 1949

LAWRENCE GAINSBURY
b. 1947

HELENE STEIN

m. 1970

ELAINE CAPLAN

m. 1971

PHILIP GAINSBURY
b. 1950

MARILYN BESNER
b. 1957

JONATHAN BESNER
b. 1958

CHARLES BESNER
b. 1960, d. 2021

MICHAEL GAINSBURY
b. 1958, d. 1983

ROCHELLE JOANNE GAINSBURY
b. 1959

CODA

GAIL COOK JOHNSON ——— m. 2017 ——— **NEIL BESNER**

LEGEND

m. married   // divorced   d. deceased